15 —

ART NOUVEAU LAMPS AND FIXTURES

ART NOUVEAU LAMPS AND FIXTURES

of James Hinks & Son

Christopher Wray

ARCH CAPE PRESS

NEW YORK

ART NOUVEAU LAMPS AND FIXTURES
was originally published in 1907 as
Electric Fittings
The Manufacture of James Hinks and Son Ltd.
Birmingham; Gt Hampton Street
London: 148 Charing Cross Road

This 1989 edition published by Arch Cape Press,
a division of dilithium Press, Ltd,
distributed by Crown Publishers, Inc.,
225 Park Avenue South,
New York, New York 10003.

ISBN 0-517-67883-7

Printed and bound in Hong Kong

h g f e d c b a

Acknowledgements

I would like to thank the following for their invaluable assistance and contributions to this book: Peggy Vance, of Bestseller Publications, for making it all possible; Joyce Fellows, of the Local Studies Department of the Birmingham Reference Library, for her historical research; and Michael Binns of Crossharbour Communications, for editorial guidance.

CW.

Introduction

THROUGHOUT man's existence, the type and style of lighting used has been determined by the technology and resources available at the time. For the first six thousand years of recorded history, people depended chiefly on animal or vegetable fat or beeswax as their source of interior light.

The fuel was either liquid, for lamps such as those found in the royal tombs of Ur, or solid, in the form of tallow. In both cases the flame was exposed, constituting a flickering fire hazard. With tallow candles there was a further problem, as Shakespeare noted when he wrote of 'the smoky light that's fed with stinking tallow'.

In extremis, light sources could be exotic. Newfoundland fishermen burned dogfish tails, while the American Indians used what they called 'candle fish'. Shetland Islanders thrust wicks down the throats of stormy petrels and ignited them. Others found that penguins made useful standard lamps.

By the nineteenth century the most commonly used fuels were colza oil and whale oil. In 1781 John Miles had invented the 'bird fountain oil feed', which kept the oil at the same effective level in the reservoir and ensured an even flow of oil to the flame. At about the same period the development of better wicks and the introduction of glass chimneys had ensured the superiority of oil lamps over candles as a light source.

It is widely assumed that in the second half of the nineteenth century first there were oil lamps, then there were gas lamps and electricity followed gas. While this is broadly true, it masks the extent to which the three forms co-existed as each was developed and improved. There was a frenzy of invention in the period, with literally thousands of patents being taken out as manufacturers invented or improved their products. There was also considerable cross-fertilisation of design elements, as existing designs for oil lights were adapted to gas and those for gas lights adapted to electricity. The choice of energy source was often conditioned by the prevailing circumstances. Gas and electricity were only available in the larger towns of Western Europe and the eastern seaboard of the United States, the areas where much of the world's lighting was manufactured. Most of the world was only equipped for oil lighting until well into the twentieth century. Many outlying areas of England were only electrified during the 1960s.

With the discovery in Pennsylvania in 1860 of plentiful supplies of bituminous shale and coal, from which paraffin could be refined, American paraffin became readily available in Europe. This was nearly odourless and smokeless, and burnt with a cleaner flame, making it a far more agreeable fuel than any other.

In 1865 Joseph Hinks of Birmingham patented the duplex burner, doubling the

amount of light an oil lamp could produce. The duplex burner consisted of two parallel wicks about ⅛ inch apart. At the time it was considered that a paraffin lamp with a Hicks duplex burner was the ideal light source. Indeed, many confident Victorians would make even grander claims for the duplex burner. In 1897 the Birmingham Magazine of Arts and Industries claimed that the duplex burner 'must have a momentous influence upon the physical comfort, and also intellectual and moral progress of the world'. The duplex burner became the foundation of Hinks' success as a producer of functional but decorative interior lighting.

Oil lamps of great beauty were made from combinations of metals, ceramics or glass. They varied in degrees of complexity: from the simple light used by the small house holder or flat dweller, to large and elaborate oiloliers (oil lit chandeliers) for use in a ballroom or grand lobby. They continued to pose intractable problems in their operation, however, and in their design limitations. The reservoirs continually had to be topped up, as the oil spots on the soft furnishings of a paraffin-lit room would testify. The components and function of the lamp also largely determined its shape. All oil lamps require a reservoir and a chimney and they all have to stand vertically.

For many years during the nineteenth century it was anticipated that gas would eventually replace oil. The first gas company in London, the National Light and Heat Company, was set up in 1804 by a German named F A Winsor, who claimed that gas was 'more congenial to the lungs than oxygen' and 'absolutely non-explosive'. The financial activities of the company were quite as fraudulent as the marketing and the National Light and Heat Company went spectacularly bust. The capital costs of setting up the gasworks and laying the piping, not to mention a considerable amount of trial and error as producers and users got to grips with the explosive qualities of gas, meant that gas did not come into widespread use until late in the century.

The superiority of gas over oil as a fuel for lighting was eventually established with the invention in 1893 of the incandescent gas mantle by Count Auer von Welsbach. When fitted onto an existing burner, von Welsbach's mantle produced a bright white light. The leap in quality was no less than that produced by Joseph Hinks' duplex burner thirty years before.

The use of gas posed different design problems. As the gas was supplied through piping, the light source had to be in a fixed position. It also required piping to convey the gas to the burner, a chimney or some kind of protection for the flame, a vertical mantle and a stopcock which had to be accessible so that the light could be turned on or off.

9

As with gas, it had long been thought that electricity could be used as a lighting fuel. In 1808 Sir Humphrey Davey had demonstrated his carbon arc lamp, in which electricity sparked across a gap between two carbon pencils, at the Royal Institution in London. The arc lamp, however, posed apparently insurmountable problems. At the time there was no regulator which would maintain the carbon pencils at an unchanging distance from one another as they quickly burnt away. Second, limitations in the generators of the time meant that only one arc lamp could be put on one circuit. Third, the harsh white light produced by arc lamps was far too bright for domestic use and appeared impossible to reduce.

In the second half of the century, attention concentrated on an alternative means of using electric power. It had been found that a carbon filament suspended between two poles inside a glass bulb would glow when an electrical current was passed through it. The problem here was to create a vacuum inside the bulb so that the filament would not oxidise and blacken the glass. This was overcome in 1865 when Hermann Sprengel invented a mercury vacuum pump which could reduce the air pressure in vessels to sufficiently low levels to enable them to be used as light bulbs.

In the late 1870s one of those strange scientific coincidences occurred, where two unconnected people arrive at the same conclusion at virtually the same time. In 1878 Sir Joseph Swan in England had invented an electric light bulb that would burn for two hours. In 1879, quite independently, the American Thomas Alva Edison invented a bulb that would burn for forty hours. The two became locked in bitter correspondence about who got there first and why, until growing competition from others led them to set up a commercial alliance in 1883 with the formation of the Edison & Swan United Electric Company Limited.

Although electricity and town gas therefore became available within a very short period of time, it was not until the early part of the twentieth century that the advantages of electricity became readily apparent. In the intervening years gas and electricity grew side by side.

In design terms electricity offered numerous advantages over gas and oil. All an electric light requires in order to function is an input cable, an output cable and a bulb. In fact, many electric lights drew, and still draw, much of their inspiration from gas lighting. The wall mounted swing arm lamps so popular in the late 1980s were originally designed as gas lamps.

At the turn of the century design was undergoing an explosion of invention and experimentation similar to that in science and technology. The Great Exhibition of 1851 had not only shown the British public the modern

wonders of the world, it had also demonstrated how unpleasant many of them looked.

While economic forces ensured the continuation of the Industrial Revolution, many people were uneasy about its social effects. The English Pre-Raphaelite movement sprang from a desire for relief from the effects of urbanisation and mass production. William Morris, concerned for the nobility and integrity of the craftsman's role in society, turned away from painting to concentrate upon household decoration. He maintained that the artist should design and oversee the production of common household objects. Such activity would also have the virtue of educating the working men who used these artefacts. The Arts and Crafts movement that followed drew intensively from Nature, plants in particular.

But the organic and leafy designs of the Arts and Crafts movement were as nothing to the hothouse growth of Art Nouveau. Decoration was inspired by the twisting forms of branches, creepers, leaves, flowers, entomology and the female form. Art Nouveau was also intensely new, liberating artists and designers from the shackles of the real or imagined traditions of the past.

Known as Art Nouveau in England, the movement was known as the Modern Style in France, Stile Liberty in Italy, Jugendstil (after the Munich magazine Jugend) in Germany and Sezessionstil in Austria. The movement was in fact a broad church, incorporating many styles from chintzy Japonaiserie to the austere geometric forms of Charles Rennie Mackintosh that prefigure the Bauhaus style of the 1920s.

The movement found its champions across Europe and in the United States. Gaudí's Temple in Barcelona is deliriously ornamented. In Belgium Paul Hankar, Horta, and van de Velde created the 'whiplash line', while writers such as Lemonnier, Maeterlinck and Verhaeren made Brussels the centre of the fin-de-siècle Symbolist movement. The entrance to the Hotel van Eetvelde in the Avenue Palmerston in Brussels, designed by Victor Horta, is a light and airy triumph of the Art Nouveau style, making playful use of the new materials of the nineteenth century, glass and iron.

Art Nouveau was strongly informed by the graphic art of painters such as de Feure, Alphonse Mucha and Aubrey Beardsley. Everywhere across Europe pale and languid ladies with white shoulders and breasts were depicted among creepers and serpents, often on posters extolling the virtues of soap, automotive products or bicycles.

A central principle of Art Nouveau was that consistency of design should run from the exterior of the building itself, through the furnishings right down to the inkpot on the desk in the study. Attention to the design of household objects was unprecedented.

In 1884 Emile Galle inaugurated his cabinet workshop in Nancy. Galle's design criteria were simple. Furniture had to be logically constructed. Its form was to be determined by its function (this may now seem surprising in view of the ornamentation of some of the furniture Galle created). 'In so far as concerns the shaping of the frame,' wrote Galle, 'we have but a simple choice between traditional contours and those taken from flora and fauna'. Galle and the others of the Ecole de Nancy chose the flora and fauna.

The Art Nouveau designers turned their attention not only to the furniture but also to the wall fabrics and papers, tapestries, stained glass windows, jugs, bowls, clocks and ornaments, and to details such as the door handles and hinges. The style took to the streets on the façades of houses in Paris, Brussels and the industrial towns of northern Italy, and under the streets, in the Paris Metro.

It was inevitable that designers would apply their skills to the new medium of electric lighting. A basic question confronting all of them was what to do about the bulb: cover it or leave it exposed for its novelty value. Galle and Tiffany, in their love of twilight themes, tended to mask the bulb, seeking effect in the illumination of their ornate glass shades.

Of all the manufacturers of Art Nouveau lighting, Louis Comfort Tiffany was perhaps the most luxuriant. Trained as a painter, he began using glass as a medium for his painting. He began experimenting with colours in the making of glass, developing his own techniques for making what he called 'favrile' glass. By 1906 the Tiffany studios listed over 400 models of oil and electric lamps and employed more than 200 people. Designs incorporated peonies, wisteria, poinsettia, rambling roses, lilies, toadstools, tulips and female figures. Tiffany insisted on the highest quality regardless of cost. Lamp bases were made of cast bronze. Every part of the lamp was hand finished. The designers of Art Nouveau had come a long way from the ambitions of the Arts and Crafts movement to bring spiritual uplift to the working classes.

The lights of James Hinks and Son are more workaday than this. Hinks was a manufacturer of good quality lighting that ordinary people could afford. The first record of Hinks is in 1847, when he was described as a die sinker, stamper and piercer at 69 Newhall Street, Birmingham.

The foundation of Hinks' success was the invention of the duplex oil burner, patented by Joseph Hinks in 1865. Hinks patented a wide range of duplex burners, which varied in the degree of sophistication of their mechanisms for raising the wick and snuffing the flame. Hinks duplex burners were supplied to lampmakers throughout the world. Tiffany used Hinks burners in his oil lamps.

Hinks incorporated the duplex burner in his own range of lighting. In 1871 James Hinks visited India to launch his lighting there. He established a special range of lighting for India, including the 'Punkah burner' and the 'Star of India'. Hinks established a virtual monopoly in India; his lights are still to be found there, as well as in Australia, South Africa and elsewhere round the world.

Hinks' Birmingham factory in Great Hampton Street was a four storey building covering an acre of ground. He also had a trade showroom at 148 Charing Cross Road in London as well as a consumer outlet in Bond Street.

Following the success of their oil lights, Hinks turned energetically to the production of gas and electrical lighting. The catalogue reproduced in these pages deals exclusively with electrical lights. First printed in 1907, it already contains hundreds of different lighting designs. It was aimed at the trade. As the preface says:

> Owing to the very rapid growth of our Electrical Fittings Branch, we have endeavoured, in producing this elaborate catalogue, to place before our clients such beautifully finished drawings that it will enable those who cannot spare the time to pay a visit to our Manufactory, or London Showroom to form as good an idea of the various designs and finishes as is possible without actually seeing the articles themselves.

With the growth of Empire and export trade, catalogues assumed great importance to Hinks, other producers such as Sherwoods, and great wholesalers such as Falk, Stadelmann, whose wares were branded with the name Veritas. Clients were often thousands of miles away. Catalogues were vital in communicating product information to clients. These clients would convey their orders telegraphically. Falk, Stadelmann developed an elaborate system, known as the S-code, to ensure that clients could telegraph their orders in a minimum number of words.

The preface to Hinks' catalogue gives an indication of the company's markets and the circumstances in which it operated. The company boasts a complete electric plant at the Charing Cross Road showroom, supplying the electricity to light the premises but also enabling the company to demonstrate to potential clients how electrical power worked and what was needed to procure it. In particular the catalogue appeals to architects and electrical engineers, offering free estimates for lighting buildings, churches and ships.

All designs (except those in wrought iron) are offered in polished brass, bronzed brass, electroplate, nickel-plate, antique copper, oxidised silver and antique brass. Customers are strongly advised to adhere to standard patterns. Too many special orders would create headaches for

the supplier. Customers returning crates in good condition within one month of delivery would be credited with the costs of packaging.

The lights in the catalogue were drawn with pen and ink and reproduced with colour added at the print stage. Some of the shades were reproduced photographically. Today, lighting suppliers give their products names. Hinks simply allocated a serial number to each with a brief description of the material and the dimensions. Only in the case of the more elaborate products is there anything more ('Large 100-Lt Electrolier, in Polished Brass. Specially suitable for Theatres, Halls & Public Buildings').

Most Hinks lights in the catalogue are made from sand cast polished brass, although black iron, copper and oxidised silver are also depicted. In many cases the bulb (tipped at the end) protrudes beyond the glass shade. Occasionally no shade is offered at all. Perhaps the novelty of electric light justified leaving the bulb visible. Where the bulb is hidden, the shade is generally made from tasselled fabric. In many

of the more obviously Art Nouveau lights the wiring, insulated with gold silk thread, is also outside the body of the light, perhaps because the wiring was considered of sufficient interest itself.

The lights presented in the 1907 catalogue will have been the accumulation of several years' designs. By no means all of them are in the Art Nouveau style. There are brackets with formal Victorian shades and table lamps that owe more to monumental neo-Classicism than anything else.

Hinks' catalogue is the statement of a confident and vigorous trading company at the beginning of the twentieth century. Some of the designs shown are still in use. Others have disappeared, perhaps only temporarily. The catalogue has the authentic feel of an age that passed with the Great War. James Hinks & Son only survived briefly into the new era. In 1925 the company was taken over by Falk, Stadelmann, which itself ceased trading in the 1970s.

Plate 1

E 1261, E 1271, E 1279. Ornate polished brass wall brackets
with clear and coloured pineapple glass shades.
E 1261 is a standard swan neck bracket decorated with acanthus leaf.
These designs have been adapted from designs for gas brackets.

E 1046. Elaborate polished brass wall bracket with open petal glass shade.
The shade leaves the tipped light bulb exposed.

E 1047. Strongly traditional Victorian polished brass bracket
with a cut glass pineapple shade.

E 1261—Polished Brass.
Spread - 7in.

E 1046—Polished Brass.
Spread - 12in.

E 1271—Polished Brass.
Spread - 10in.

E 1047—Polished Brass.
Spread - 7in

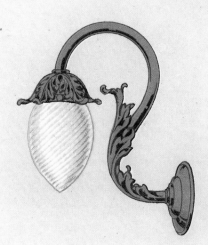

E 1279 – Polished Brass.
Spread - 9in.

Plate 2

E 1048. Polished brass wall bracket with leaf motifs and vaseline glass shade.

E 1073. Polished brass wall bracket with white glass shade.

E 1227. Polished brass double wall bracket with translucent blue onyx coloured glass shades. The base of the bracket is very similar to that in lamp number E 1048 (above). A stylised oak leaf motif masks the joint between the two lamp branches.

E 1278, E 1288. Polished brass two and three branch wall brackets with diamond optic vaseline globe glass shades. The globes are held by large galleries with leaf motifs.

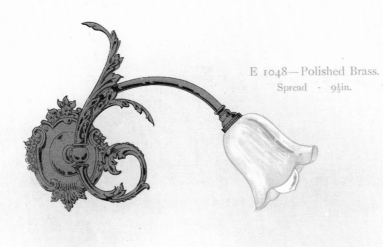

E 1048—Polished Brass.
Spread - 9½in.

E 1278—2-Lt. Polished Brass.
Projection - 10in.
Spread - 12in.

E 1073—Polished Brass.
Spread - 6½in.

E 1227—2-Lt.
Polished Brass.
Spread - 9in.
Projection - 8in.

E 1288—3-Lt. Polished Brass.
Projection - 12in.
Spread - 12in.

Plate 3

E 1080. Mirror with red plush velvet frame supporting a three armed light bracket.
The mirror is in bevelled plate glass with thumbprint highlights.
The body of the bracket is in polished brass.
The leaf decoration is copper.

E 1009. Empire style mirror with two armed light bracket in brass and copper,
shown without shades.

E 1011. Two armed polished brass bracket with tulip shades on a
wooden wall patrice.

E 1080—3-Lt.
Polished Brass & Copper,
with Bevelled Mirror &
Plush Velvet Frame.
Spread · 9in.

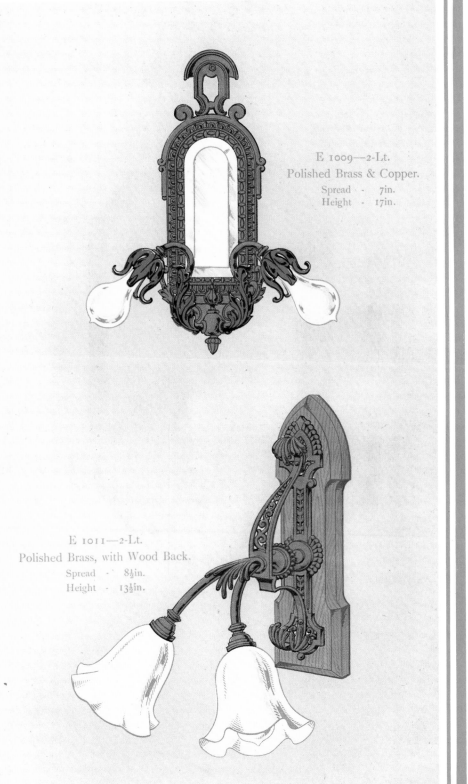

E 1009—2-Lt.
Polished Brass & Copper.
Spread · 7in.
Height · 17in.

E 1011—2-Lt.
Polished Brass, with Wood Back.
Spread · 8½in.
Height · 13½in.

Plate 4

E 1128. Clean-lined Art Nouveau bracket in polished brass,
supporting a pendant white glass langham shade suspended
on its gold silk thread wiring.

E 1123. Oxidised silver neo-Gothic Art Nouveau pendant lantern
suspended from a bracket with a stylised lily motif.
The lantern is shaded by vaseline glass.

E 1124. Polished brass wall light with copper shade. The leaflike shade
is similar to the shell shades still produced today.

E 1303. Polished brass wall bracket with pendant white glass langham shade.
No attempt has been made to build the wiring into the metalwork.
The wire itself is a decorative feature.

E 1247. A wooden wall patrice supporting an Art Nouveau oxidised silver bracket
from which hangs a turquoise fabric shade with tassels.

E 1250. Large wooden wall patrice supporting an elaborate Art Nouveau
oxidised silver projecting bracket, from which hang two small green tasselled
fabric shades in the Chinese style.

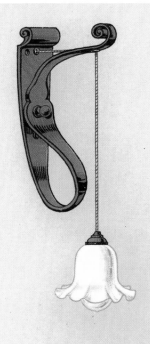

E 1128—Polished Brass.
Height - 12in.
Spread - 6in.

E 1303—Polished Brass.
Height - 10in.
Spread - 8in.

E 1123—Oxydized Silver.

With Opalescent Shade.
Height - 33in.
Spread - 10in.

E 1247—Oxydized Silver.
With Wood Back.
Height - 7in.
Spread - 6in.

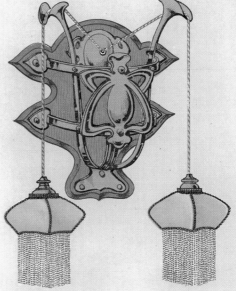

E 1250—2-Lt
Oxydized Silver.
With Wood Back.
Height - 12in.
Spread - 9½in.
Projection - 6in.

E 1124
Polished Brass & Copper.
Height - 11in.

Plate 5

E 1241. Oxidised silver wall arm on a wooden wall patrice, supporting a small,
Chinese style, red tasselled shade with a large gallery.
While bearing a distinctively Art Nouveau line,
the bracket maintains more ornate traditional influences.

E 1248. Wooden backed oxidised silver wall bracket with small,
Chinese style, red tasselled shade.

E 1104. Polished brass and copper bracket and lamp with conical vaseline shade
bearing a line optic. The straight edge of the bracket arm is unusual among
Art Nouveau forms. The shade with its spiral surround prefigures
the Vorticism of a few years later.

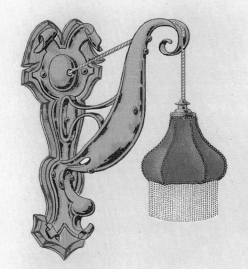

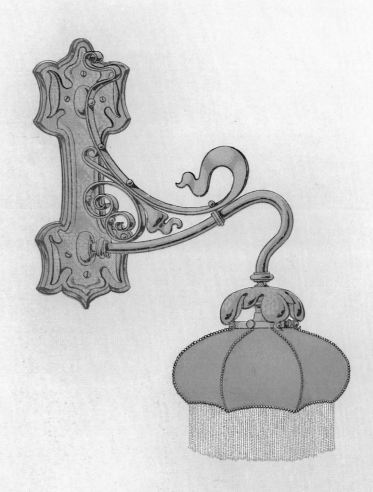

Plate 6

E 1200. Wooden wall patrice bearing a polished brass frame supporting
two pendant concave swirled frosted crystal shades
with thumbprint highlights.

E 1327. Oxidised silver base plate with two plantlike brackets supporting
pendant opalescent tulip shades.

E 1225, E 1226, E 1092. Lightly scrolled black iron wall arms with
white and opalescent shades, leaving the pointed bulb to protrude.
The arms were probably adapted from designs for gas lighting.

E 1200—2-Lt.
Polished Brass.
With Wood Back.
Height - 12in.
Spread - 12½in.

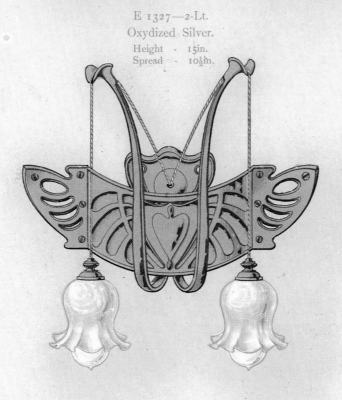

E 1327—2-Lt.
Oxydized Silver.
Height - 15in.
Spread - 10½in.

E 1225—Black Iron.
Height - 6in.
Spread - 12in.

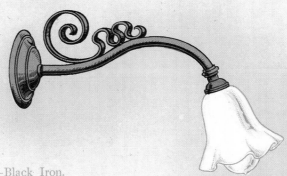

E 1226—Black Iron.
Height - 6in.
Spread - 12in.

E 1092—Black Iron.
Height - 10½in.
Spread - 13½in.

Plate 7

E 1165. Arts and Crafts black iron bracket supporting
a pendant lamp and shade.

E 1152. Black iron base holding a copper stanchion from which grows
a plantlike black iron support, from whose whiplash hangs
a small green Chinese style fabric tasselled shade.

E 1192. Black iron bracket supporting a red tasselled shade.

E 1193. This black iron bracket is more traditional than
above but the line is more stylised.
The pendant light is suspended
from a black iron loop.

E 1165—Black Iron.
Projection - 7in.
Height - 13in.

E 1192—Black Iron.
Projection - 10in.
Height - 18in.

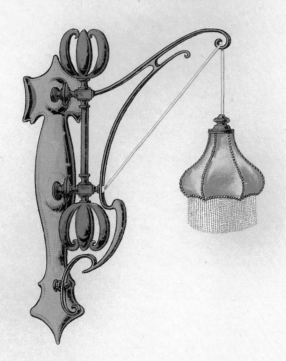

E 1152
Black Iron & Copper.
Projection - 11in.
Height - 20in.

E 1193—Black Iron.
Projection - 9½in.
Height - 18½in.

Plate 8

E 1117. Black iron wall bracket with copper bud motif and
pendant white glass petal shade.

E 1015. Black iron bracket with three branches.
The main body of the bracket has black iron leaves.
Copper corrollae surround the vaseline glass shades.
A fourth corolla surmounts the bracket.

E 1117
Black Iron & Copper.

Projection - 11in.
Height - 22in.

E 1015—3-Lt.
Black Iron & Copper.

Projection - 8in.
Height - 18in.
Spread - 10in.

Plate 9

E 1175. Oxidised silver table lamp with elaborate red shade.
The lamp body has the simple form of a candle stick.
The red fabric shade is reminiscent of nothing
so much as a lady's bustle.

E 1173. Polished brass table lamp on a tripod base. The body of the lamp is a
neo-Classical column. The red fabric shade is late Victorian.

E 1180. Polished brass table lamp with traditional yellow shade.
While still in many respects traditional in form,
the body of the lamp is buttressed by a handle.

E 1168. Oxidised copper table lamp with green shade.
The column of the lamp has a kink in it,
reflecting the increased interest in line at the close
of the nineteenth century.

E 1175—Oxydized Silver.
Height - 12 in.

E 1173—Polished Brass.
Height - 9½ in.

E 1180—Polished Brass.
Height - 12 in.

E 1168—Oxydized Copper.
Height - 12 in.

Plate 10

E 1181, E 1179. Polished brass desk lamps with red shades.

E 1178. Polished brass table lamp with green shade. Set on a tripod, the simple body of the lamp is supplemented by a single handle.

E 1183. Polished brass table lamp with a red shade. Although the upper part of the lamp stand is traditional, the lower part reveals much of the Art Nouveau interest in line. One of the three feet of the tripod curls upward to form a handle on the other side of the lamp body.

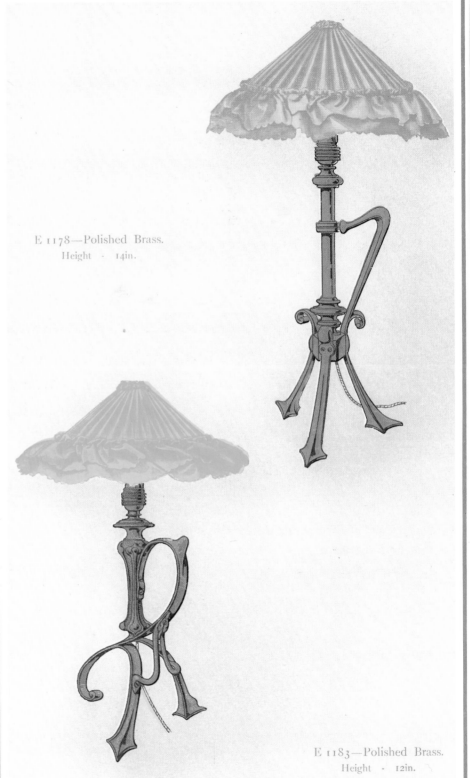

E 1178—Polished Brass.
Height - 14in.

E 1181—Polished Brass.
Height - 13in.

E 1179—Polished Brass.
Height - 12in.

E 1183—Polished Brass.
Height - 12in.

Plate 11

E 1182. Two pictures of the same polished brass lamp that may be used either as a table light or as a wall light. The circular base has three holes with which it may be screwed to the wall. A hinge allows the lamp to be inclined. As a table light, the lamp has a green coolie fabric shade. As a wall light, it has a red fabric petal shade.

E 1326. Two pictures of another polished brass lamp that may be used either as a table or as a wall light. Mounted on a tripod, this light too has a hinge with a large circular nut, allowing it to be inclined. One of the feet of the tripod has an eyelet, with which the light could be suspended from a hook on the wall.

E 1326—Polished Brass.
Height - 13in.

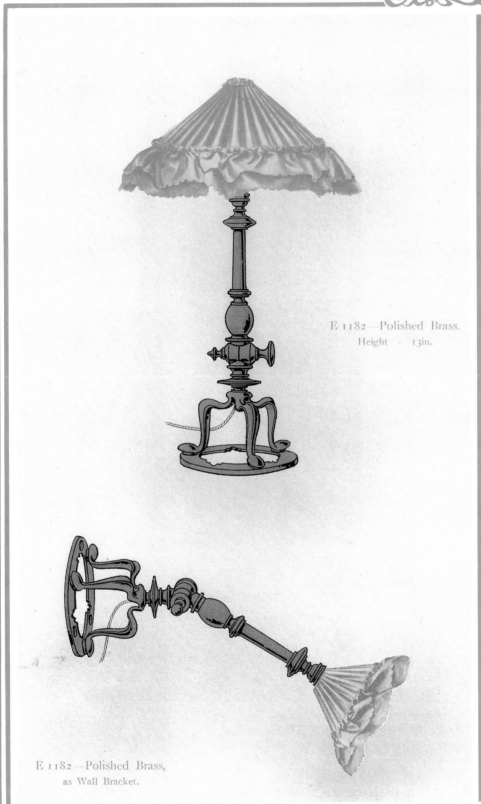

E 1182—Polished Brass.
Height - 13in.

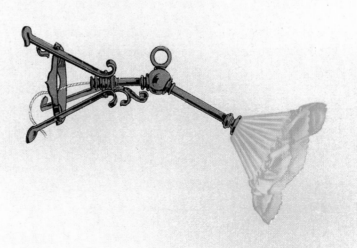

E 1182—Polished Brass,
as Wall Bracket.

E 1326—Polished Brass,
as Wall Bracket.

Plate 12

E 1170. Oxidised silver statue table lamp with an ornate green shade.
The body of the light is in the form of a robed girl standing on
an ornate mound decorated with scalloped wave patterns.
The girl is holding aloft the lamp holder with her left arm.
The wire is threaded through her right hand and then
through the waves at the base of the lamp.

E 1305, E 1306. Two oxidised silver table lamps. Although the red and green shades
are traditional and frilly, the lamp bodies are simple. The upper lamp
has the curved line familiar to the Art Nouveau style and has a hinge
at the joint of its two legs, suggesting that the lamp could
also be mounted on the wall. The lower lamp is
more austere with its straight lines.

E 1170—Oxydized Silver.
Height - 16½in.

E 1305—Oxydized Silver.
Height - 11in.

E 1306—Oxydized Silver.
Height - 11in.

Plate 13

E 1304. Oxidised silver table lamp with traditional green fabric shade.
The three legs of the lamp stand upon a tricorn base, the wire running
between the legs and threading through the base.

E 1186. Polished brass table lamp. The traditional yellow shade has been capped
with a polished brass framework. The body of the lamp is buttressed
by three brass shoulders which become the tripod upon which the light stands.
The wire is incorporated in the central body of the light.

E 1184. Oxidised silver table lamp with red shade. The three legs of the light are set
on a circular base. The base has eyelets so that the light could be mounted on a wall.
A hinge allows the lamp to be inclined.

E 1081. Ornate oxidised silver table lamp with elaborate green shade.
Drawing from mythology, the body of the light contains a woman's face
surrounded by a headdress. The body stands upon a raised platform
which itself is supported by four three-clawed feet,
each one clutching a ball.

E 1304—Oxydized Silver.
Height - 12in.

E 1186—Polished Brass.
Height - 11½in.

E 1184—Oxydized Silver.
Height - 13½in.

E 1081—Oxydized Silver.
Height - 19in.

Plate 14

E 1112. Polished brass and copper table light with a Victorian green fabric shade.
The brass body of the light is decorated by simple copper ornamentation.

E 1129. Oxidised copper and brass table light with green fabric shade.
The light rests on a tripod of three large brass feet.

E 1025. Polished brass table light with a yellow fabric shade with an exterior frame.
Although essentially simple and classical in design, the light is decorated
with asymmetrical brasswork around the base,
prefiguring the Art Nouveau style.

E 1112
Polished Brass & Copper.
Height - 17½in.

E 1129
Oxydized Copper & Brass.
Height - 14½in.

E 1025—Polished Brass.
Height - 18in.

Plate 15

E 1003, E 1086. Neo-classical oxidised silver table lamps with Corinthian columns and full skirted Victorian shades. Probably adapted for electricity from existing designs for candlesticks.

E 1003—Oxydized Silver.

Height - 15in.

E 1086—Oxydized Silver.

Height - 20in.

Plate 16

E 1078. Polished brass adjustable desk lamp with white glass shade.
The lamp is supported by an arm projecting from the column of the light.
The height of the arm is adjustable, the arm being fixed
by a thumbscrew which is tightened against the column.
Beneath the column is a tripod standing on a
hand chased cast brass tricorn base.

E 1026. Polished brass and copper table light with vaseline tulip shade.
The curved stem of the light and its shade recall the stem and flower of a plant.
The design has been elaborated with copper leaves and the tendril
of a creeper spiralling around the stem of the light.

E 1078—Polished Brass.

Adjustable to 29in.

E 1026

Polished Brass & Copper.

Height - 26in.

Plate 17

E 1212. Oxidised silver pendant lantern with a vaseline glass tubular shade. The cap on the light resembles a witch's hat.

E 1187. Oxidised silver pendant light. This is in fact the same light as the wall bracket light E 1123 on Plate 4. Here the light is offered without the bracket.

E 1198. Similar to E 1212 (left), this light is more elaborately ornamented with the whiplash line associated with Art Nouveau and is shown here in oxidised copper with a ruby optic cylinder shade.

E 1133. Polished brass and copper pendant light with a white translucent swirled peardrop glass shade.

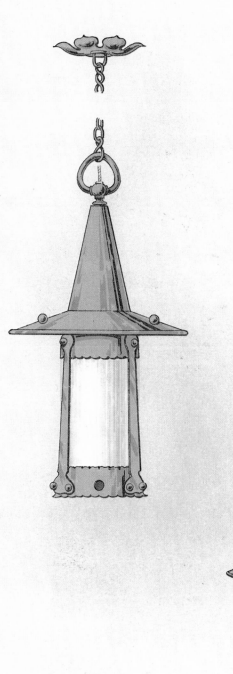

E 1212—Oxydized Silver.
5in. Opalescent Cylinder.
Spread - 12in.

E 1198—Oxydized Copper.
With 5¾in. Ruby Shaded Cylinder.

E 1133
Polished Brass & Copper.
Spread - 6½in.

E 1187—Oxydized Silver.
5in. Opalescent Shade.
Spread - 7½in.

Plate 18

E 1344, E 1343, E 1339. Although distinctively Art Nouveau
with their whiplash lines, these oxidised silver pendant lights have a minimalism
only possible in lights lit by electricity.

E 1340, E 1341. Oxidised silver pendant lamps. The tubular shades of these lights
recall the safety lamps developed by Sir Humphrey Davy for use in mines.

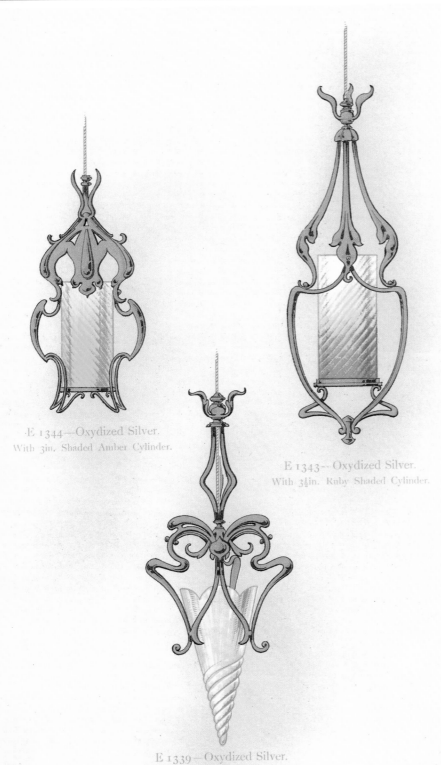

E 1344—Oxydized Silver.
With 3in. Shaded Amber Cylinder.

E 1339— Oxydized Silver.
With 4in. Taper Opalescent Shade.

E 1343— Oxydized Silver.
With 3½in. Ruby Shaded Cylinder.

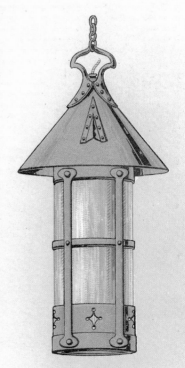

E 1340—Oxydized Silver.
With 4½in. Amber Cylinder.

E 1341— Oxydized Silver.
With 4½in. Cathedral Green Shade.

Plate 19

E 1342. Polished brass pendant light with cathedral green glass shade. Although simple in design, the lines of this light place it clearly at the turn of the century.

E 1122. Polished brass pendant light with amber glass. The simple basic design has been elaborated with motifs recalling Chinese art.

E 1342--Polished Brass.
With Cathedral Green Shade.
Spread - 8¾in.

E 1122
Polished Brass & Amber Glass.
Spread - 25½in.

Plate 20

E 1211. Black iron and polished copper pendant lamp
with a ruby tinted 5 inch cylindrical shade.

E 1126. Black iron lantern with cathedral green glass. The lantern hangs from
a solid and modern looking black iron wall bracket. There are heart motifs
in the bracket and round the top of the lantern. No wire is visible
but a wire would presumably have to run outside the bracket
and be threaded through the links of the chain.

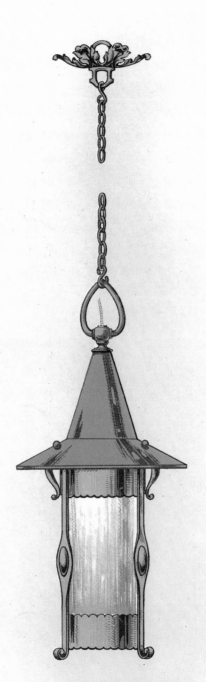

E 1211
Black Iron & Polished Copper.
Ruby Tinted 5in. Cylinder.

E 1126 Black Iron.
With Cathedral Green Glass.
Diameter - 13in.

Plate 21

E 1204. Black iron pendant light with peardrop glass shade with a swirled optic. The ironwork is highly wrought yet spare.

E 1197. Black iron and oxidised copper pendant light with a 5 inch vaseline glass cylinder shade with a diagonal optic. While the basic design of the pendant is similar to that of E 1211 (Plate 20), Art Nouveau decorative elements have been introduced, such as the whiplash line of the black iron body.

E 1167. Black iron and polished brass pendant light with pink tasselled shade. There are elements of the Art Nouveau line in the metalwork, but the shade gives the light a Chinese look.

E 1204 — Black Iron.
Spread · 6in.

E 1197
Black Iron & Oxydized Copper.
With 5in. Opalescent Cylinder.

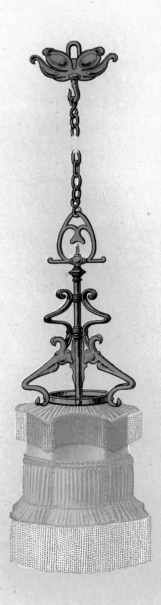

E 1167
Black Iron & Polished Brass.
Spread · 8½in.

Plate 22

E 1157. Black iron and polished copper pendant light with fabric shade.
The traditional shade reduces the modern effect of the metalwork.

E 1135. Black iron pendant light with a red tasselled shade.
The weight of the light is supported by the electric wire alone.
The shade is reminiscent of a Vesta oil lamp shade.

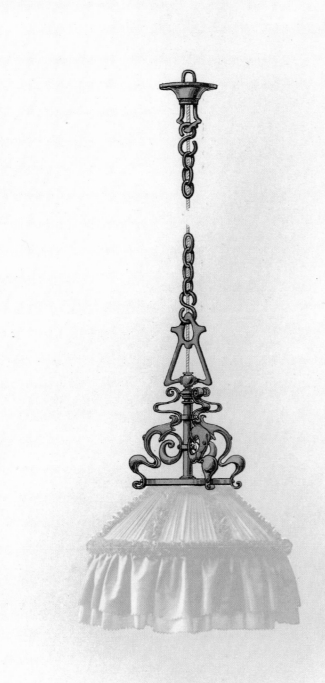

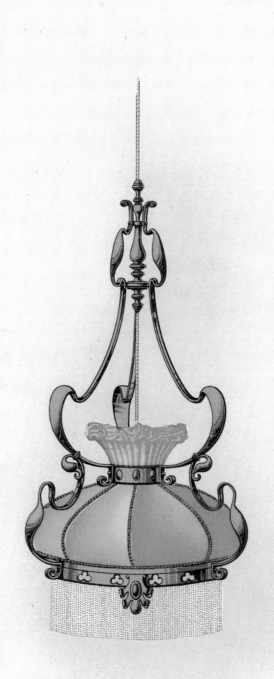

E 1157
Black Iron & Polished Copper.
Spread - 9in.

E 1135—Black Iron.
Spread - 17in.

Plate 23

E 1132. Black iron and oxidised copper chandelier supporting five lights with
cut glass shades. While the copper ring supporting the lights
has a strong Art Nouveau style, the cut glass pineapple shades
are strongly traditional.

E 1360. Black iron and oxidised copper pendant light with a tasselled opal shade.
The weight of the light is supported by three stout chains.
The body of the light is made from black iron.
Only the decorative escutcheon is in oxidised copper.
The shade was originally a Vesta oil lamp shade.
Very likely this light was designed with a view
to consuming an existing stock of
redundant oil light shades.

E 1132—5-Lt.
Black Iron & Oxydized Copper.
Spread - 24in.

E 1360—3-Lt.
Black Iron & Oxydized Copper.
18in Opal Shade.

Plate 24

E 1196. Black iron and oxidised copper lantern with an obscured flint shade. The mix of iron and copper is delicately balanced. Art Nouveau decorative elements have been introduced into what is essentially a Victorian design.

E 1161. Black iron three light chandelier with glass trumpet shades. The wiring is external to the spare body of the light. With a spread of 17 inches the light is more than three feet long and could only be used in a high ceilinged room or hallway.

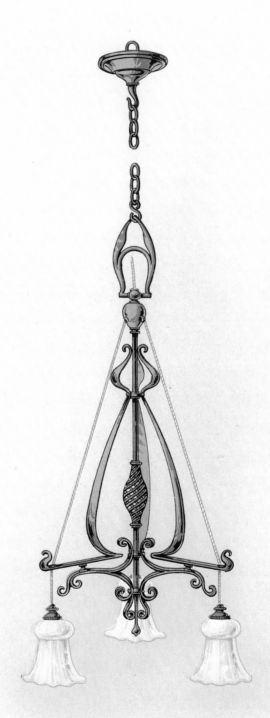

E 1196
Black Iron & Oxydized Copper.
With Obscured Flint Shade.
Spread - 11½in.

E 1161—3-Lt. Black Iron.
Spread - 17in.

Plate 25

E 1164. Three light black iron and oxidised copper chandelier with white crimped glass shades.

E 1163. Three light black iron and oxidised copper pendant fitting. The wiring of the light is external: it would have been impossible to thread wire through this design.

E 1164—3-Lt.
Black Iron & Oxydized Copper.
Spread · 17in.

E 1163—3-Lt.
Black Iron & Oxydized Copper.
Spread · 20in.

Plate 26

E 1151. Three light black iron and oxidised copper pendant fitting
with white crimped glass shades.

E 1154. Five light black iron pendant light fitting.
The wires have been threaded down the centre
of the fitting until they spread outwards
to the pendant lamps.

E 1151—3-Lt.
Black Iron & Oxydized Copper.
Spread - 18in.

E 1154—5-Lt. Black Iron.
Spread - 32in.

Plate 27

E 1195. Three light black iron and oxidised copper pendant light fitting. While the metalwork is elaborate in line and bears strong influences of Art Nouveau, the shades are staunchly Victorian.

E 1249. Two light oxidised silver wall bracket with green pendant tasselled shades. The bracket is mounted on a wooden wall patrice. The Chinese style tasselled shades are suspended from two looped stalks which project from the bracket like an insect's antennae.

E 1014. Polished copper and brass sconce with two lights. The backplate and stalks of the light are brass. The leafy decoration is beaten copper. The bulbs of the light are left bare.

E 1195—3-Lt.
Black Iron & Oxydized Copper.
Spread - 21in.

E 1249—2-Lt.
Oxydized Silver.
With Wood Back.
Height - 15in.
Spread - 9in.
Projection - 7½in.

E 1014—2-Lt.
Polished Copper & Brass.
Height - 14½in.

Plate 28

E 1310, E 1311, E 1312. Three pendant lights in polished brass. E 1310 and E 1311 have decorative vaseline glass shades. E 1312 has a glass beaded fringe.

E 1314, E 1315, E 1317. Three pendant lights in polished brass. E 1314 and E 1315 have glass beaded fringes. E 1317 has the same vaseline glass shade as E 1310. The minimal nature of the designs of these six lights was only made possible by the use of electricity as a lighting medium.

E 1310
Polished Brass.
3¼in. Fitting.

E 1311
Polished Brass.
3¼in. Fitting.

E 1312
Polished Brass.
3¼in. Fitting.

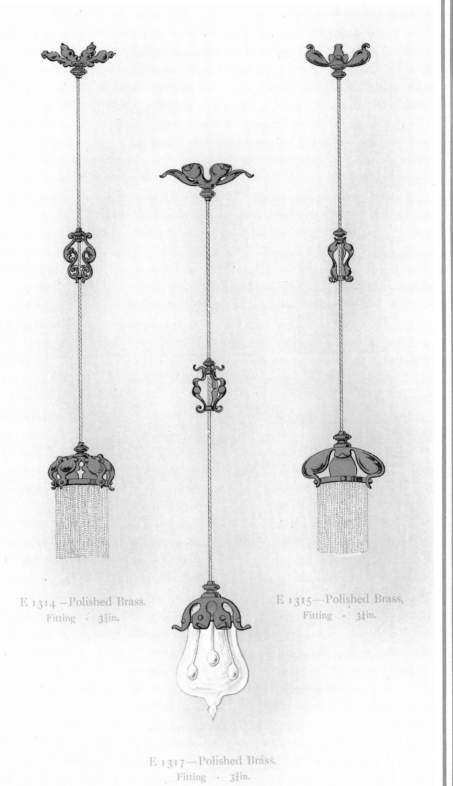

E 1314 —Polished Brass.
Fitting · 3¼in.

E 1315—Polished Brass,
Fitting · 3¼in.

E 1317—Polished Brass.
Fitting · 3¼in.

Plate 29

E 1320. Rise and fall light in china and polished brass with a glass coolie shade.
The china counterweight is filled with lead shot to provide ballast.

E 1321. Polished brass rise and fall light with a tasselled coolie shade.
Both these lights would be suitable for illuminating
a working area such as a sewing table.

E 1322. Elaborately complex rise and fall light with a canting arrangement allowing
the angle of the light to be adjusted. The weight of the light is supported by its
electrical wiring as far as the bracket holding the canting mechanism.

E 1321—Polished Brass.
With 10in. Shade & Ring.

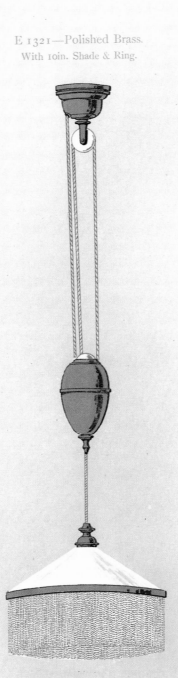

E 1320
China & Polished Brass Mounts.
With 10in. Shade.

E 1322—Polished Brass.
With Canting Arrangement.

Plate 30

E 1105. Three light rise and fall pendant in oxidised copper and brass. The rather traditional silk shade is ringed with a brass frame.

E 1072. Three light polished brass rise and fall light with an elaborate magenta frilly silk shade. The ceiling hook and shade holder are decorated with acanthus leaf motifs.

E 1105—3-Lt.
Oxydized Copper & Brass.
Spread - 24in.

E 1072
3-Lt. Polished Brass.
Spread - 9in

Plate 31

E 1238. Rise and fall pendant light in oxidised silver and copper.
The oxidised silver counterweight is decorated with a stylised leaf motif.
The base holding the shade is decorated with a copper cylinder.

E 1237. Three light oxidised silver rise and fall pendant light with a green silk shade.
Although the basic shape of this light is actually fairly traditional,
the detailing has many of the characteristics
of the Art Nouveau movement.

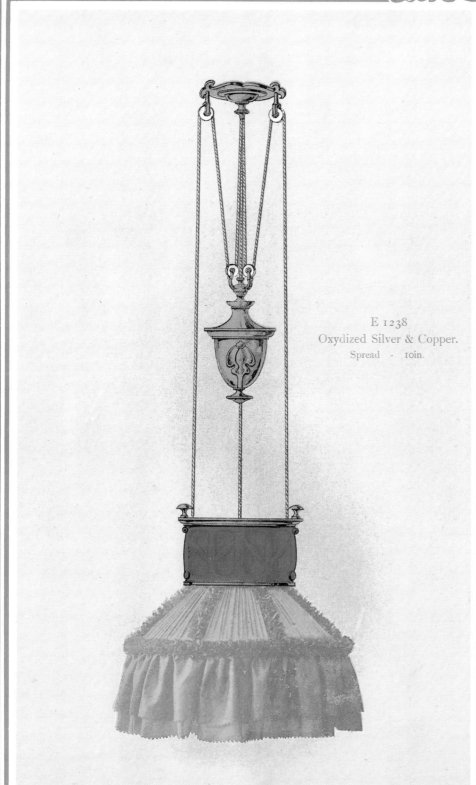

E 1238
Oxydized Silver & Copper.
Spread - 10in.

E 1237—3-Lt. Oxydized Silver.
Spread - 24in.

Plate 32

E 1359. Heavy oxidised silver three light rise and fall pendant lamp.
The gallery supports a red silk shade, whose glass beading
is suspended from a lower ring.

E 1332. Elaborate seven light rise and fall pendant fitting in oxidised silver
and copper. This could almost be seen as two light fittings put together.
The ceiling mount supports four vaseline glass shades. The three light rise and
fall fitting has a blue silk shade with clear glass beads.
Projecting from beneath the shade is a handle to be grasped
when pulling the light downwards or pushing it upwards.

E 1359—3-Lt. Oxydized Silver.
Spread - 20in.

E 1332—7-Lt.
Oxydized Silver & Copper.
Spread - 24in.

Plate 33

E 1127. Spare two light polished brass rise and fall dressing table pendant fitting with vaseline glass shades. The crest on the ring between the two lights is reminiscent of a thistle.

E 1329. Modern looking two light oxidised silver and polished copper rise and fall dressing table pendant lamp with white glass shades. The centre of the light and the counterweight are decorated with polished copper bosses.

E 1127—2-Lt. Polished Brass.
Spread - 18in.

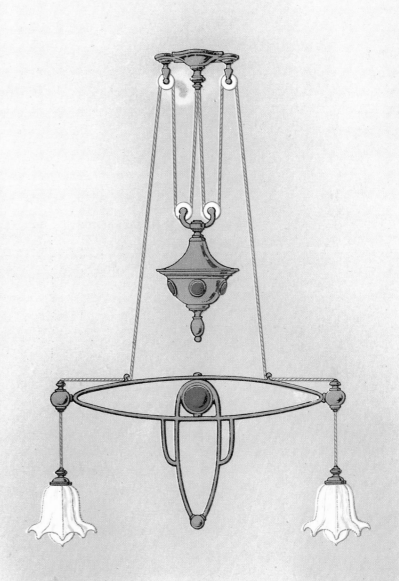

E 1329—2-Lt. Oxydized Silver
& Polished Copper.
Spread - 20in.

Plate 34

E 1215. Two light oxidised silver rise and fall dressing table pendant lamp with white glass shades. A cut crystal ball is incorporated into the base of the light. The modern looking base itself contains decorative elements drawn from lily leaves.

E 1328. Two light polished brass and copper rise and fall dressing table pendant lamp with vaseline shades. The polished brass structure of the light is decorated with polished copper heart motifs.

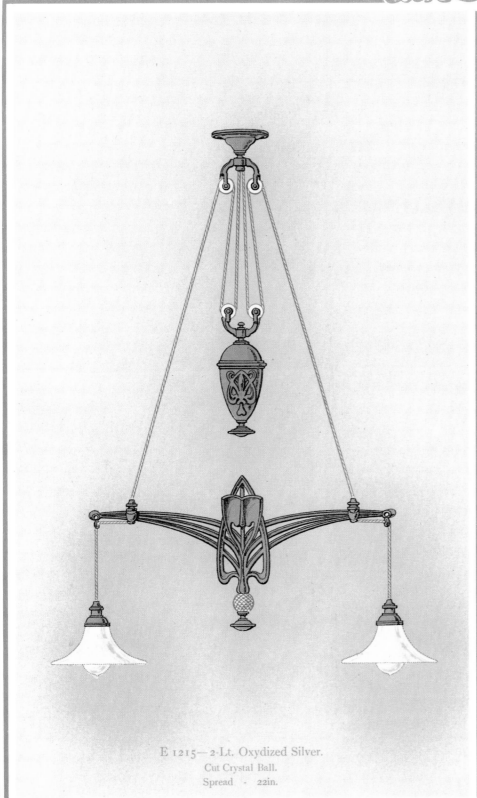

E 1215—2-Lt. Oxydized Silver.
Cut Crystal Ball.
Spread - 22in.

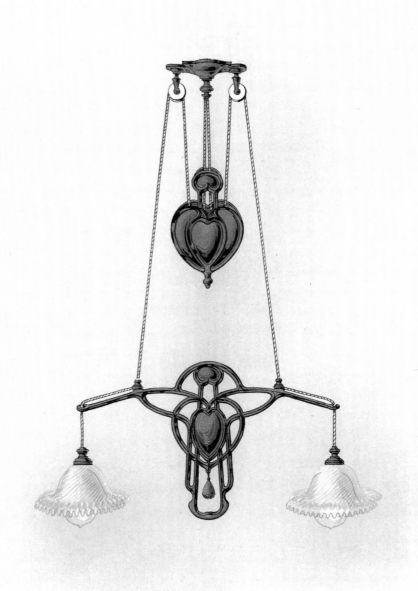

E 1328
2-Lt. Polished Brass & Copper.
Spread - 20in.

Plate 35

E 1059, E 1058, E 1057. Three two light polished brass pendant lamps with glass shades. The wiring is incorporated in the brass tubing. These are very typical examples of early electric light fittings.

E 1027. Four light polished brass and copper pendant light. Shown here without shades, the lampholders are masked by stylised acanthus leaves.

E 1059—2-Lt. Polished Brass.
Spread - 18in.

E 1058—2-Lt. Polished Brass.
Spread - 22in.

E 1057—2-Lt. Polished Brass.
Spread - 22in.

E 1027—4-Lt.
Polished Brass & Copper.
Spread - 8in.

Plate 36

E 1020. Four light polished brass pendant fitting with acanthus leaf motifs
and vaseline shades which leave the extremities of the bulbs bare.

E 1029. Elaborate four light polished brass and copper pendant fitting.
The brass tube running from the ceiling mount is conventional until
it reaches a bud from which issues a riot of further buds and leaves.
The four bulbs hang on their own wiring and are decorated with copper shades.
Brass beads have been threaded onto the wires to create festoons.

E 1020—4-Lt. Polished Brass
Spread - 14in.

E 1029—4-Lt.
Polished Brass & Copper.
Spread - 12½in.

Plate 37

E 1017. Three light polished brass pendant fitting with white glass shades. The fitting is suspended from Hinks' patent chain. The chain was designed for use with
electricity or gas. Electrical wiring could be run down one side of the chain and gas tubing down the other.

E 1012. Typically Edwardian three light polished brass pendant fitting with vaseline glass shades. The fitting is suspended on a polished brass chain.

E 1017—3-Lt. Polished Brass.
With Patent Chain.
Spread - 21in.

E 1012—3-Lt. Polished Brass.
Spread - 18in.

Plate 38

E 1076. Four light polished brass pendant fitting with vaseline glass shades having a vertical optic. Two lights sprout from the arms of the fitting, two are attached to a knuckle joint at the base. The fitting is suspended from Hinks' patent chain, suitable for use either with gas or with electricity.

E 1024. Spare but conventional three light polished brass pendant fitting, decorated with acanthus leaf motifs and with white glass shades. The right angles at which the lampholders are set suggest that this was originally a gaslight fitting.

E 1076—4-Lt. Polished Brass.
With Patent Chain.
Spread - 18in.

E 1024—3-Lt. Polished Brass.
Spread - 24in.

Plate 39

E 1035. Three light polished brass pendant fitting with white glass shades that leave the bulbs exposed.

E 1034. Three light cast, hand chased and polished brass pendant fitting with white glass shades. The light branches grow from stylised acanthus leaves. Stylised lions' heads decorate the central globe.

E 1035—3-Lt. Polished Brass
Spread · 10in.

E 1034—3-Lt. Polished Brass.
. Spread · 18in.

Plate 40

E 1075. Conventional Victorian polished brass three light fitting
with cut crystal pineapple shades. The fitting is suspended
from Hinks' patent chain.

E 1065. Richly Victorian three light polished brass fitting with glass shades.
The fitting is suspended from Hinks' patent chain. The brass was cast
and then hand chased before polishing.

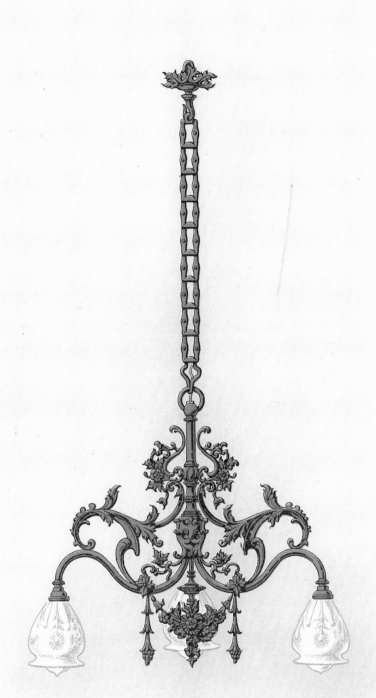

E 1075—3-Lt. Polished Brass.
With Patent Chain.
Spread - 15in.

E 1065—3-Lt. Polished Brass.
With Patent Chain.
Spread - 20in.

Plate 41

E 1121. Art Nouveau three light polished brass pendant fitting with vaseline glass shades. This light is much more experimental than those in the preceding few pages. The designer has taken every advantage of the electrical medium the light would use.

E 1131. Three light oxidised silver pendant fitting with white glass shades having diamond optics. The oxidised silver is put to elaborate use around a relatively simple central stem.

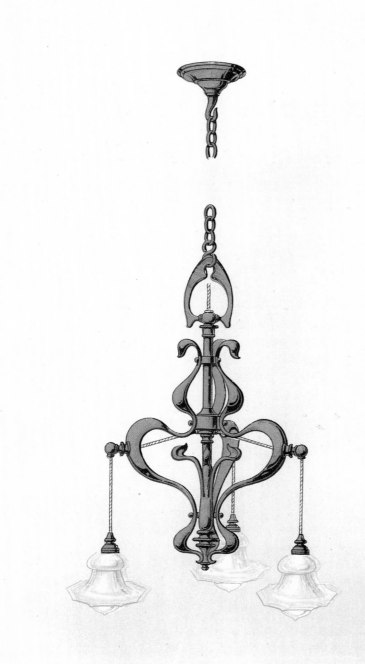

E 1121—3-Lt. Polished Brass
Spread - 15in.

E 1131—3-Lt. Oxydized Silver
Spread - 15in.

Plate 42

E 1113. Four light polished brass pendant fitting with white pendant shades with diamond optics.

E 1363. Three light oxidised silver pendant fitting with vaseline pendant shades.

E 1113—4-Lt. Polished Brass.
Spread · 14in.

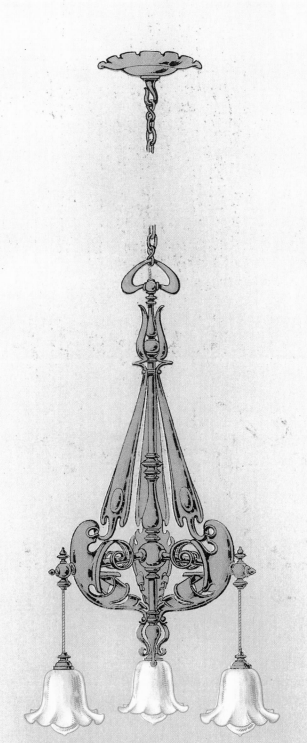

E 1363—3-Lt. Oxydized Silver.
Spread · 16in.

Plate 43

E 1139. Three light oxidised copper pendant fitting with small turquoise
Chinese style tasselled shades. Each fabric panel of the shades was hand sewn onto
the frame. The wiring passes down from the ceiling into the upper body of the fitting.
It then emerges from three holes in the sphere to run downwards to the shades
which are held outwards by three copper buttresses.

E 1145. Three light polished brass pendant fitting suspended from
a polished brass chain. The vaseline glass shades are held by rigid brass branches
emerging from the body of the fitting.

E 1139—3-Lt. Oxydized Copper.
Spread - 18in.

E 1145—3-Lt. Polished Brass.
Spread - 16in.

Plate 44

E 1331. Magnificent five light polished brass and oxidised copper fitting suspended from a Hinks patent chain. The rectangular lanterns have panes of cathedral green glass: four of them are suspended from the corners of a rigid oxidised copper square with Art Nouveau motifs. The fifth lantern hangs through the centre of the square. The rectangular links of Hinks' patent chain are at one with the right angles of the rest of the design. Only the leafy decoration above the globe from which the corner chains hang stands out. Perhaps the company had no cleaner cut component in stock so it made shift with what it had.

E 1330. Six light polished brass and oxidised copper pendant fitting with vaseline shades. Made of the same materials as E 1331 (left), this light is much more conventional, as a quick glance shows.

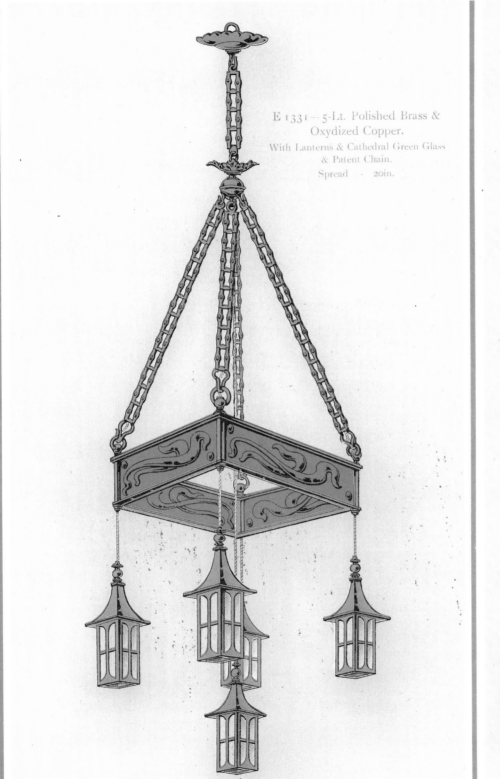

E 1331—5-Lt. Polished Brass &
Oxydized Copper.
With Lanterns & Cathedral Green Glass
& Patent Chain.
Spread - 20in.

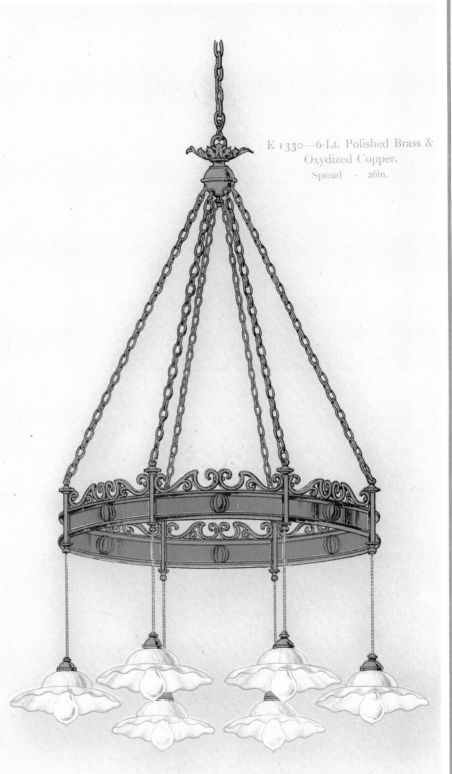

E 1330—6-Lt. Polished Brass &
Oxydized Copper.
Spread - 26in.

Plate 45

E 1354. Oxidised silver five light pendant fitting with vaseline glass daffodil shades. With a spread of 26 inches, the light is only supported by the electric wiring hanging from the ceiling. There is even an extra piece of ornamentation half way down the cable.

E 1060. Very conventional three light polished brass pendant fitting, suspended on a Hinks patent chain. The prismatic shades are unusual and rarely found.

E 1354—5-Lt. Oxydized Silver.
Spread - 26in.

E 1060—3-Lt. Polished Brass.
With Patent Chain.
Spread - 16in.

Plate 46

E 1068. Empire style three light polished brass pendant fitting, suspended on a polished brass chain. The three white shades are fed from rigid branches.

E 1115. Three light polished brass pendant fitting with white shades on rigid brass branches.

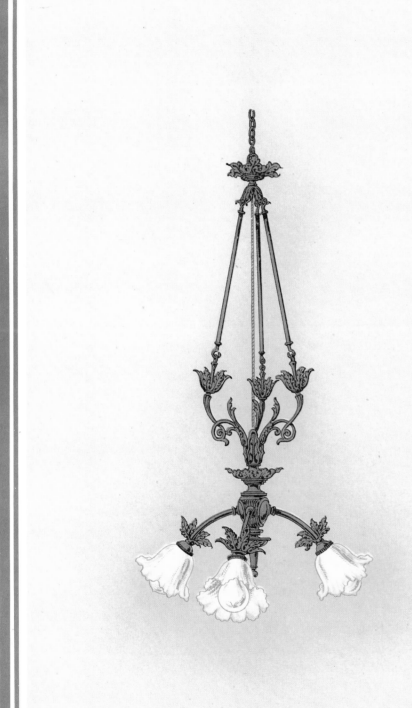

E 1068—3-Lt. Polished Brass.
Spread - 11in.

E 1115—3 Lt. Polished Brass.
Spread - 17in.

Plate 47

E 1069. Oxidised silver three light pendant fitting suspended on a Hinks patent chain, also in oxidised silver. The white glass shades are mounted at the end of rigid branches. This fitting is unusual among Hinks' pendant lights. The nude female figure standing on entwined branches with her arm aloft supporting the main body of the light makes the whole structure asymmetrical.

E 1100. Charming three light polished brass pendant fitting with white glass shades. Between and above each shade sits a tiny nude cherubic figure twirling a foulard above its head.

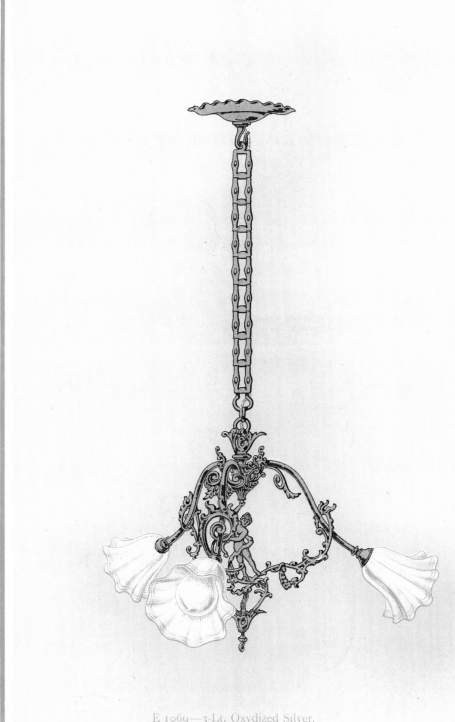

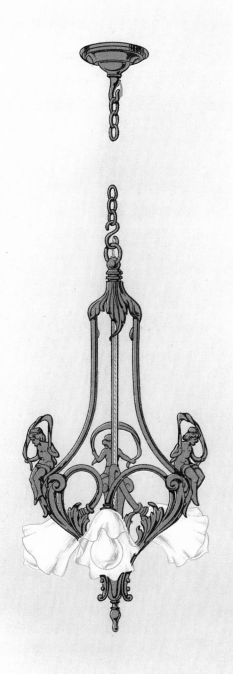

E 1069—3-Lt. Oxydized Silver.
With Patent Chain.
Spread · 17in.

E 1100—3-Lt. Polished Brass
Spread · 13in.

Plate 48

E 1064. Highly ornate four light oxidised silver pendant fitting suspended on a
Hinks patent chain. The lamps have white glass tulip shades.

E 1355 and E 1356. Traditional wall bracket and matching pendant fitting,
both in oxidised silver. Both fittings have rigid branches and vaseline glass shades.
Both fittings have cast swags hanging between the arms.
The two light bracket is mounted on a wooden wall patrice.
At the centre of each fitting is a classical urn motif.

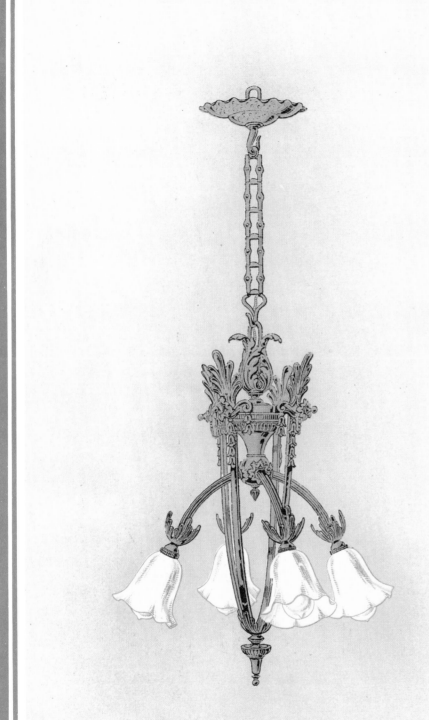

E 1355 —2-Lt. Oxydized Silver.
With Wood Back
Spread - 14in.

E 1356 — 5-Lt. Oxydized Silver.
Spread - 23in.

E 1064 —4-Lt. Oxydized Silver.
With Patent Chain.
Spread - 15in.

Plate 49

E 1357 and E 1358. Matching two light sconce and five light pendant lamp, both in oxidised silver. The sconce is mounted on a wooden wall patrice. Both fittings are in a simple and elegant classical style based around the motif of an urn from the top of which the branches sprout. Only one other style of fitting in this catalogue has crystal festoons and droppers. There is a cut crystal mount at the base of the pendant. The elaborately flared bulbs are most unusual.

E 1102. Asymmetrical polished brass pendant fitting, from which hang five bulbs with white glass shades.

E 1357—2-Lt. Oxydized Silver.
With Crystal Festoons & Droppers,
& Wood Back.
Spread - 15in.

E 1358—5-Lt. Oxydized Silver
With Crystal Festoons,
Droppers, & Cut Mounts.
Spread - 21in.

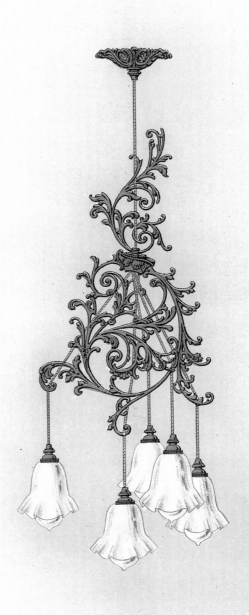

E 1102—5-Lt. Polished Brass.
Spread - 12in.

Plate 50

E 1061. Five light polished brass and oxidised silver pendant fitting on a Hinks patent chain. The fitting is based upon an S-shape. The top of the S fits through the ring attached to the bottom of the chain. The body of the S is decorated with acanthus leaves and a looping tendril. Three of the light branches curve downwards at the bottom of the S. A fourth branch rises, subdividing to feed the other two lights. A nude female figure scantily draped sits precariously upon the fourth branch at the centre of the fitting, nonchalantly holding the tendril above with her left hand as she reaches towards one of the lights. Perhaps her confidence derives from her oxidised silver wings.

E 1108. Twenty-two light electrolier in oxidised silver with a repoussé copper dome which calls to mind the cupolas of the Brighton Pavilion. Beneath the dome and in the centre of the fitting is a large cut crystal globe. At the top of each of the four pairs of struts holding the construction together is a human face surrounded by ornamentation. Five and a half feet high, with a spread of three feet, this massive piece was suitable for only the grandest of hotel or theatre foyers. Imperial Victoriana with added electricity.

E 1061
5-Lt. Polished Brass &
Oxydized Silver.
With Patent Chain.
Spread - 18in:

E 1108
22-Lt. Oxydized Silver & Copper.
Repoussé Dome & Cut Crystal Globe in Centre.
Height - 66in.
Spread - 36in.

Plate 51

E 1150. Sinuous three light polished brass pendant fitting with small hand sewn green fabric tasselled shades in the Chinese style.

E 1146. Three light oxidised silver pendant fitting with small hand sewn red fabric tasselled Chinese style shades.

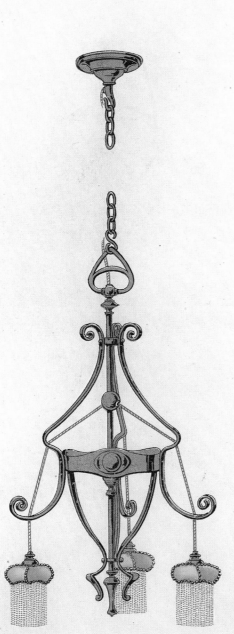

E 1150—3-Lt. Polished Brass.
Spread - 13in.

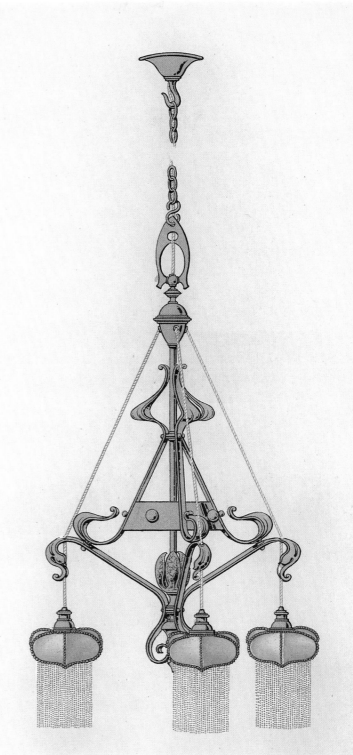

E 1146—3-Lt. Oxydized Silver.
Spread - 17in.

Plate 52

E 1149. Three light polished brass pendant light fitting with turquoise Chinese style tasselled shades. Stylised human faces decorate the cross struts of the fitting.

E 1155. Three light polished brass pendant fitting with vaseline shades.

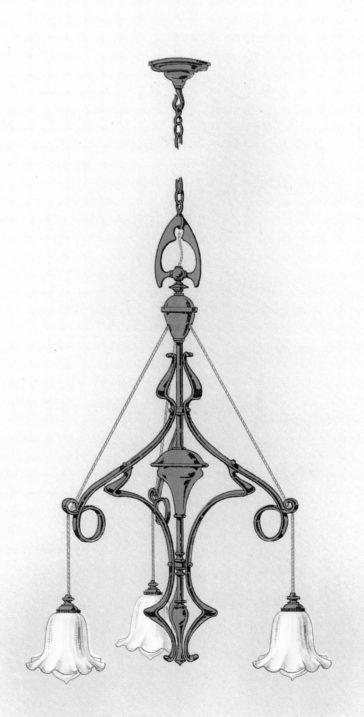

E 1149—3-Lt. Polished Brass.
Spread · 15in

E 1155—3-Lt. Polished Brass.
Spread · 18½in.

Plate 53

E 1148. Three light polished brass pendant fitting with hand sewn hanging orange tasselled shades in the Chinese style.

E 1176. Three light polished brass pendant fitting with hand sewn hanging crimson tasselled shades in the Chinese style.

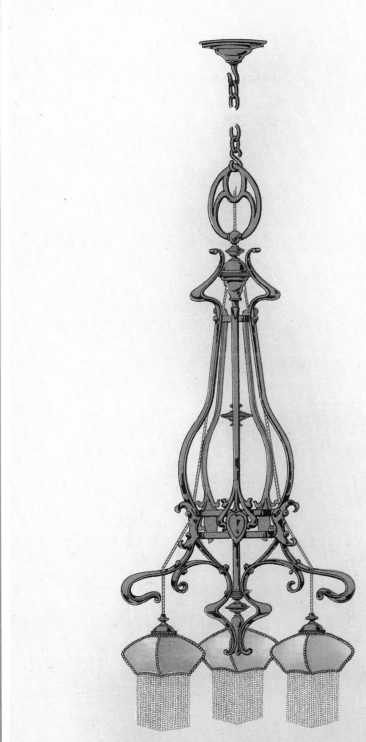

E 1148—3-Lt. Polished Brass.
Spread - 13in.

E 1176—3-Lt. Polished Brass.
Spread - 22in.

Plate 54

E 1208. Three light polished brass pendant fitting
with vaseline glass shades.

E 1189. Three light polished brass pendant fitting
with red fabric cabbage leaf shades.

E 1208—3-Lt.
Polished Brass.
Spread · 22in.

E 1189—3-Lt.
Polished Brass.
Spread · 15in.

Plate 55

E 1190. Four light oxidised silver pendant fitting with vaseline glass peardrop shades
with a swirled optic. While three of the lights hang beneath the fitting,
the fourth is located within its body.

E 1156. Four light oxidised silver pendant fitting with white shades.

E 1190—4-Lt.
Oxydized Silver.
Spread - 15in.

E 1156—4-Lt. Oxydized Silver.
Spread - 22in.

Plate 56

E 1295. Seven light oxidised silver pendant fitting. Four of the lights are suspended beneath the fitting within the cut glass pineapple shades. The other three are contained within the cut bowl in the centre.

E 1234. Simple three light polished brass pendant fitting, suspended from its own wiring, with vaseline glass shades. A typical early electric pendant.

E 1098. Three pale blue fabric shades are suspended from a structure similar to two drawn longbows set one through the other at right angles.

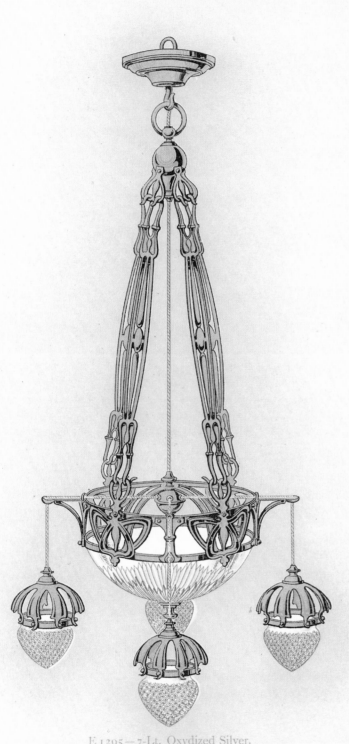

E 1234—3-Lt. Polished Brass.
Spread - 12in.

E 1295—7-Lt. Oxydized Silver.
With 12in. Cut Bowl in Centre.
Spread - 18in.

E 1098—3-Lt. Polished Brass.
Spread - 14in.

Plate 57

E 1120 and E 1119. Two small polished brass pendant fittings, each with four bulbs.
E 1120 is shown with white glass shades with teardrop overlay optics.
Those on E 1119 are in vaseline glass.

E 1103. Polished brass pendant fitting with a large orange silk shade.
The shade is surmounted by a cast brass eagle with its wings outstretched
and its head turned to one side.

E 1094. Polished brass pendant fitting with a vaseline shade.
The wire from which the fitting is suspended is ornamented
with curled and rippling brasswork.

E 1120—4-Lt. Polished Brass.
Spread - 6in.

E 1103—Polished Brass.
Spread - 10in.

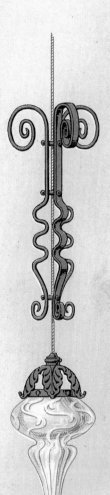

E 1119—4-Lt. Polished Brass.
Spread - 9in.

E 1094—Polished Brass.
Spread - 5in.
Fitting - 3¼in.

Plate 58

E 1097. Spare but convoluted three light polished brass pendant fitting with small Chinese style green tasselled shades. The emphasis on line makes this an austere form of Art Nouveau.

E 1028. Polished brass and copper three light pendant fitting.
The bare bulbs have a ruff of spikey copper leaves.
Acanthus leaves are built into the body of the light.

E 1097—3-Lt. Polished Brass.
Spread · 10½in.

E 1028—3-Lt. Polished Brass & Copper.
Spread · 12in.

Plate 59

E 1099. Elegant minimalist Art Nouveau rise and fall pendant fitting in polished brass. The exposed wire is an integral part of the fitting's final form. The mass of the bulb, lampholder and shade is balanced by a brass counterweight.

E 1019. Three light polished brass and copper pendant fitting. The bare bulbs protrude through gaps in the copper acanthus leaves.

E 1031. Oxidised silver and polished brass pendant fitting. The electrical wiring passes through the top of an oxidised silver crescent moon. Between the horns of the moon hangs the bulb. The lampholder is surrounded by a polished brass gallery in the form of a star.

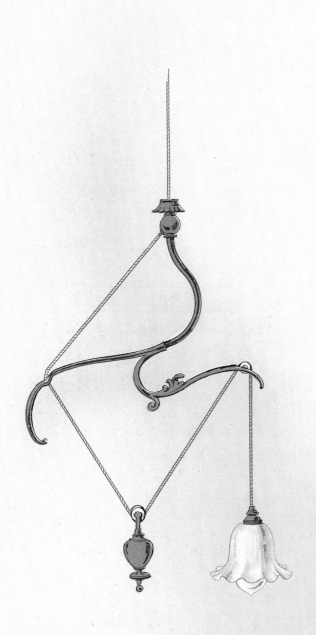

E 1099—Polished Brass.

Spread - 16½in.

E 1019—3-Lt.

Polished Brass & Copper

Spread - 16½in.

E 1031

Oxydized Silver & Polished
Brass.

Height - 13in.
Spread - 10in.

Plate 60

E 1070. Oxidised silver and polished brass pendant fitting with a vaseline glass shade. The polished brass figure of a scantily draped nude girl sits inside the oxidised silver crescent. Like a naked mountaineer sitting on a ledge, with her right hand she holds the electrical wiring descending through the top of the crescent, while her left pays the cable out to the lampholder below.

E 1062. Oxidised silver and polished brass pendant fitting with a vaseline glass shade. The body of the light is formed by a polished brass nude female figure. She tucks her right leg upwards and backwards, like a hurdler with the unfair advantage of a large pair of oxidised silver wings on her shoulders. The wiring is passed through her lowered right hand and upwards through her raised left hand before it is poured down to the lampholder below.

E 1008. Large polished brass four light pendant fitting with a white glass Vesta shade originally designed for use with oil lights. The flat circular body of the light is tasselled. The three secondary lights have vaseline glass shades.

E 1070—Oxydized Silver
& Polished Brass.
Height · 15in.
Spread · 7in.

E 1062—Oxydized Silver
& Polished Brass.
Height · 13in.
Spread · 10in.

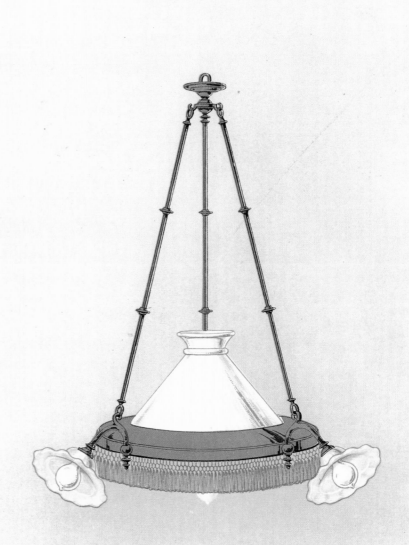

E 1008
4-Lt. Polished Brass.
With 18in. Opal Shade.
Height · 46in.
Spread · 30in.

Plate 61

E 1166. Tall and narrow polished brass pendant fitting
with a traditional red silk shade.

E 1232. Three light oxidised silver pendant fitting. The fitting is suspended
from three twisted oxidised silver struts which each pass through a fleur de lys
punched out of a crested plate. A green silk tasselled shade is incorporated within
the body of the fitting, which is capped by a thin flat opal disc.
The electrical wiring passes through the centre of the disc.

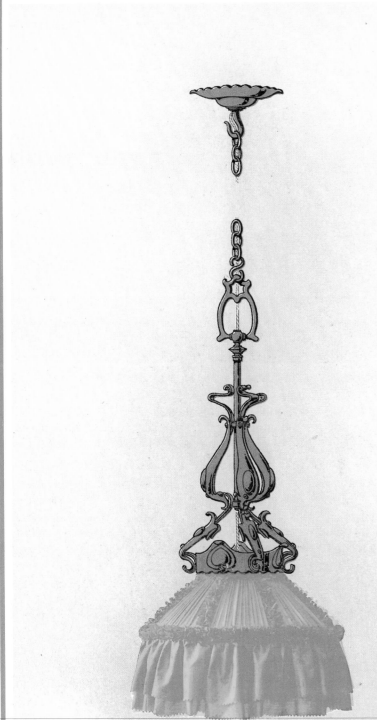

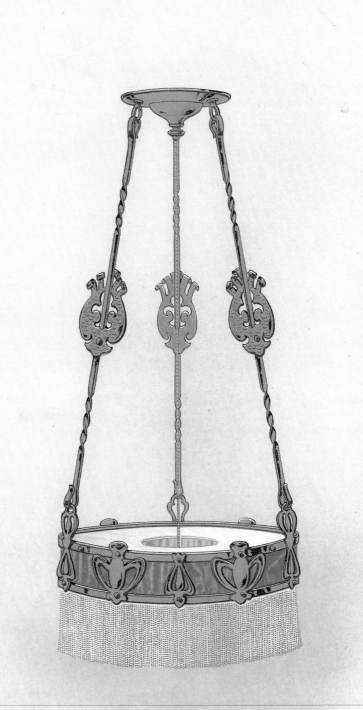

E 1166—Polished Brass.

Height - 44in.
Spread - 8½in.

E 1232 - 3-Lt. Oxydized Silver.

With Opal Disc.

Height - 40in.
Spread - 18in.

Plate 62

E 1235. Oxidised silver pendant light with Art Nouveau motifs
and a pale blue traditional silk shade.

E 1361. Six light oxidised brass pendant fitting with a red silk tasselled shade
incorporated into the body. Similar to the fitting E 1232, an additional
three bulbs are suspended from the crown from which the three chains
supporting the body of the fitting hang.

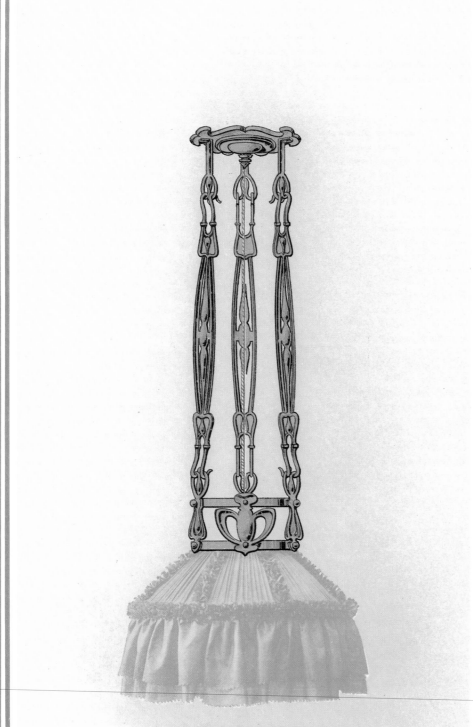

E 1235—Oxydized Silver.
Height - 30in.
Spread - 8in.

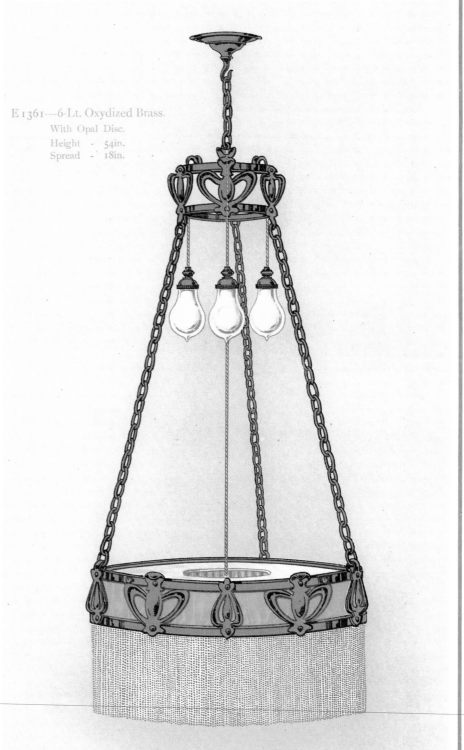

E 1361—6-Lt. Oxydized Brass.
With Opal Disc.
Height - 54in.
Spread - 18in.

Plate 63

E 1224. Oxidised silver and copper four light pendant fitting with hanging pale blue tasselled shades in the Chinese style. In the centre of the main body of the light is an embossed convex copper plate.

E 1136. Oxidised copper pendant fitting with a large red traditional shade with glass beads differently cut and threaded to form the triangular pattern. The copper fitting has the angularity of the Art Nouveau line.

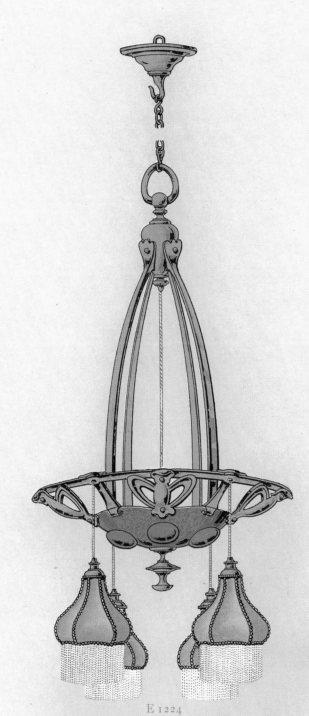

E 1224

Oxydized Silver & Copper.

Height - 42in.
Spread - 16½in.

E 1136—Oxydized Copper.

Spread - 9in.

Plate 64

E 1346. Four light oxidised copper pendant fitting with small orange tasselled shades in the Chinese style. The body of the pendant is supported by the four electrical cables, which are separated at the ceiling plate.

E 1137. Polished brass pendant fitting, supported on its electrical wiring, with an ornate silk shade with glass beading differently cut and threaded to form the pattern.

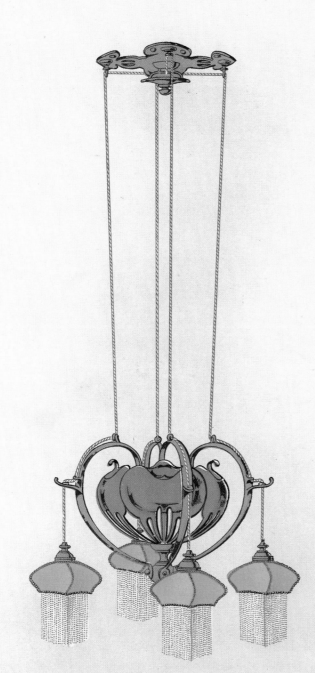

E 1346
4-Lt. Oxydized Copper
& Polished Brass.
Spread - 15in.

E 1137—Polished Brass.
Height - 19½in.
Spread - 10½in.

Plate 65

E 1138. Polished brass pendant fitting with a large red shade with a glass bead fringe. The fitting has a strong and simple line.

E 1090. Large three light black iron pendant fitting with wrought ornamentation and vaseline glass shades.

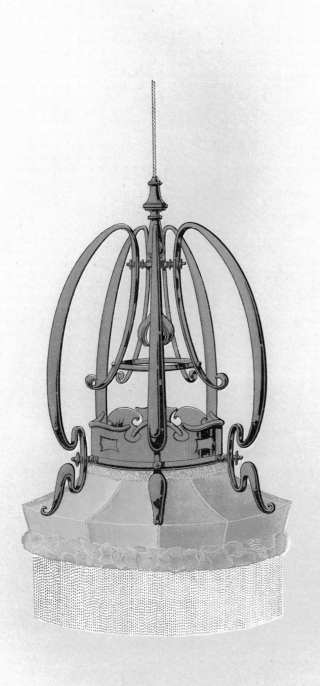

E 1138—Polished Brass.
Height - 24in.
Spread - 16½in.

E 1090—3-Lt. Black Iron.
Height - 45in.
Spread - 22½in.

Plate 66

E 1095. Black iron and polished copper pendant fitting with a single bulb partly masked by a crimped white glass shade. The ironwork is formed into leaves, tendrils and stalks. At the ends of the two stalks are polished copper buds.

E 1023. Black iron three light pendant fitting with motifs of acanthus leaves and coiled tendrils and crimped white glass shades.

E 1095
Black Iron & Polished Copper.
Length over Scrolls, 15in.

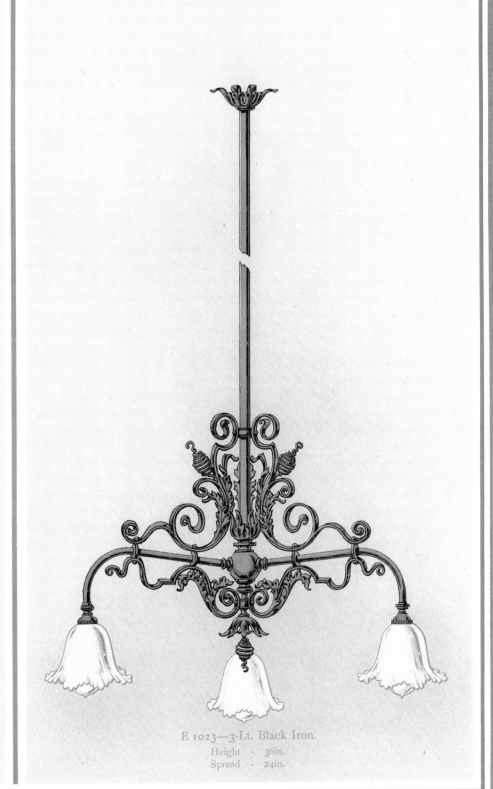

E 1023—3-Lt. Black Iron.
Height - 36in.
Spread - 24in.

Plate 67

E 1089. Ten light black iron pendant fitting with crimped vaseline glass shades.

E 1109. Three light black iron pendant fitting. While the essential proportions of the fitting are traditional, all the detail has been stylised in forms somewhere between the Arts and Crafts movement and Art Nouveau. The vaseline glass shades have a swirling diagonal optic.

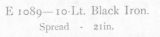

E 1089—10-Lt. Black Iron.
Spread - 21in.

E 1109—3-Lt. Black Iron
Spread - 22in.

Plate 68

E 1022. Large, scrolled, leafy and ornate black iron five light pendant
with crimped white glass shades. This may be derived
from an original design for a gaslight.

E 1369. Polished brass banker's lamp with a brass shade holder, shown here
with a green glass shade. The base of the light is perforated to allow it to be bolted
to a table, counter or partition.

E 1367. Polished brass banker's lamp with drophead and vaseline glass shade.
Slightly higher than E 1369 (above), the base of this light
is also perforated to allow permanent fixing.

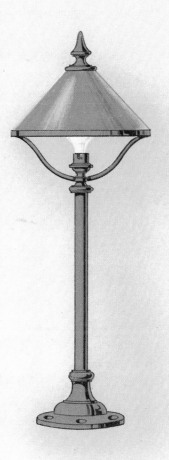

E 1369—Polished Brass.
With 9in. Shade Holder.
Height - 16in.

E 1367—Polished Brass.
Height - 21in.

E 1022—5-Lt. Black Iron.
Spread - 22in.

Plate 69

E 1110, E 1281, E 1285 and E 1264.
Ceiling lights in black iron (E 1110) and polished brass.

E 1273, E 1053 and E 1045.
Ceiling lights in polished brass and (E 1045) polished brass and polished copper.

E 1110—Black Iron.
Spread - 9in.

E 1281—Polished Brass.
Spread - 5½in.

E 1273—Polished Brass.
Spread - 5¼in.

E 1053—Polished Brass.
Spread - 7½in.

E 1285—Polished Brass.
8in. Plain Bowl.
Spread - 11½in.

E 1264—Polished Brass.
Spread - 5¼in.

E 1045
3-Lt. Polished Brass & Copper.
Spread - 10in.

Plate 70

E 1036 and E 1044. Leafy three branched ceiling lights in polished brass
and (E 1044) polished copper and brass.

E 1111. Three branched ceiling light in polished brass.
The base of the light is decorated with acanthus leaf motifs.

E 1036—3-Lt. Polished Brass
Spread   9in.

E 1044
3-Lt. Polished Copper & Brass.
Spread - 9½in.

E 1111—3-Lt. Polished Brass.
Spread - 12in.

Plate 71

E 1043. Six light polished brass and copper ceiling fitting
with acanthus leaf decoration.

E 1282. Ornate three light oxidised pendant fitting. The heavy brass was cast and
then hand chased before the fitting was oxidised. The vaseline glass pineapple shades
have a diagonal swirled optic. The lampholders are held in the mouths of elaborate
dolphins, joined to the central body with their tails.

E 1043
6-Lt. Polished Brass & Copper.
Spread - 14in.

E 1282—3 Lt. Oxydized Silver.
Spread - 12in.

Plate 72

E 1067 and E 1018. Two polished brass three light ceiling fittings with acanthus leaf motifs and glass shades.

E 1063. Ornate Arts and Crafts polished brass three light pendant fitting with vaseline glass tulip shades.

E 1067—3 Lt. Polished Brass
Spread · 8in.

E 1018—3-Lt. Polished Brass.
Spread · 14in.

E 1063—4-Lt. Polished Brass.
Spread · 17in.

Plate 73

E 1349. Art Nouveau oxidised silver three light pendant fitting with hanging vaseline glass teardrop shades with elaborate optics.

E 1350. Oxidised silver and copper Art Nouveau five light pendant fitting with hanging vaseline glass peardrop shades with teardrop optics.

E 1350
5-Lt. Oxydized Silver & Copper.
Spread - 19in.

E 1349—3-Lt. Oxydized Silver.
Spread - 18in.

Plate 74

E **1209.** Polished brass ceiling fitting with three lights partially covered by white crimped glass shades.

E **1348.** Art Nouveau polished brass ceiling light with a single bulb.

E **1216.** Oxidised silver circular ceiling fitting with a fifteen inch cut crystal bowl and lustres.

E **1284.** Oxidised copper ceiling fitting with a vaseline glass shade.

E **1283.** Polished brass circular ceiling fitting with a cut crystal bowl.

E 1216—3-Lt. Oxydized Silver.
With 15in. Cut Crystal Bowl and Lustres.
Spread - 24in.

E 1209—3-Lt. Polished Brass.
Spread - 15in.

E 1284—Oxydized Copper.
Spread - 11in.

E 1348—Polished Brass.
Spread - 12in.

E 1283—Polished Brass.
12in. Cut Crystal Bowl.
Spread - 19½in.

Plate 75

E 1347. Futuristic Art Nouveau oxidised silver ceiling light
with a seven inch crystal bowl.

E 1351. Four light oxidised silver ceiling fitting with crystal festoons,
drops and mounts. The simple lines of the metalwork contradict
the ornate luxuriousness of the crystal.

E 1338 and E 1335. Two polished brass three light pendant fittings
with vaseline glass shades. The designs on the shades of
E 1335 are etched into the glass.

E 1347—Oxydized Silver.
7in. Crystal Bowl.

E 1338—3-Lt. Polished Brass
Spread - 12in.

E 1351—4-Lt. Oxydized Silver,
With Crystal Festoons, Drops, & Mounts.
Spread - 11½in.

E 1335—3-Lt. Polished Brass.
Spread - 12in.

Plate 76

E 1334. Six light Art Nouveau oxidised silver wraparound,designed for application on columns. The spread of the fitting would depend upon the breadth of the column and the basic model would be adjusted to order.

E 1336. Six light polished brass pendant fitting on a polished brass chain. The bulbs are partially masked by white crimped glass shades.

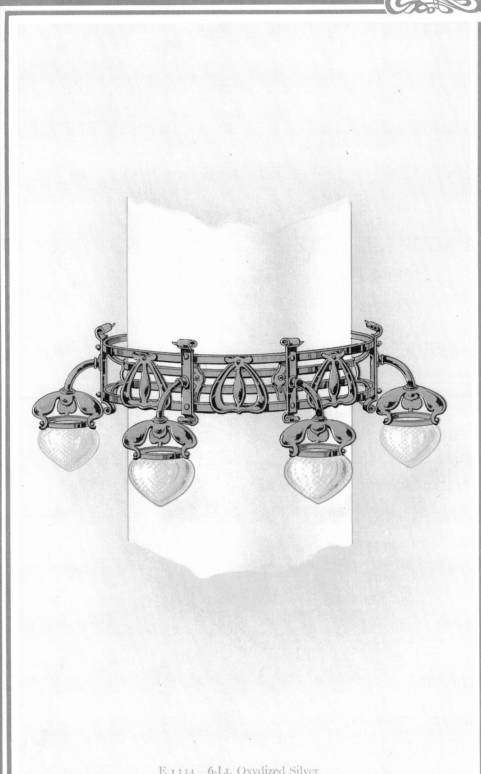

E 1334 —6-Lt. Oxydized Silver
Spread to order.

E 1336—6-Lt. Polished Brass.
Spread · 24in.

Plate 77

E 1337. Eighteen light polished brass pendant fitting on a polished brass chain. The bulbs are masked by vaseline crimped glass shades.

Large one hundred light electrolier in polished brass. As the catalogue says, this fitting is 'specially suitable for Theatres, Halls & Public Buildings'.

This massive fitting (unfortunately no dimensions are given) is suspended from the ceiling by a rigid polished brass tube. At the top of the fitting, the regal elements to be detected in other products in the catalogue have here been developed into a full blown imperial crown. Beneath the crown, eight struts support the main body of the fitting. An ornate brass ring, decorated with acanthus leaves and surmounted with a mass of lamp branches, tapers beneath before opening out again with a smaller growth of acanthus leaf motifs supporting another cluster of bulbs.

The electrolier shown here is the product of an age of mighty excess. It is easy to imagine bearded princes and plutocrats in white tie and tails gathering beneath this bombastic piece of interior architecture to discuss the relative merits of the stock prices, horseflesh and concubines of the period.

No catalogue number is given for this piece. It would have been especially made to order and is included in the catalogue to indicate Hinks' willingness to take on any project no matter how large or complex.

E 1337—18-Lt. Polished Brass.
Spread · 28in.

Large 100-Lt. Electrolier,
in Polished Brass.
Specially suitable for Theatres,
Halls, & Public Buildings.
Prices upon application.

Plate 78

E 1071. Starkly simple six light polished brass billiard table fitting with green glass coolie shades. The two extremities are supported by two polished brass struts attached to the rigid brass tube from which the fitting is suspended.

E 1364. Six light polished brass billiard table fitting with green glass coolie shades framed by decorative brasswork to protect them from damage. Instead of the simple struts of the preceding fitting (E 1071), the extreme central arms of this fitting are supported by richly wrought brass decorated with acanthus leaf motifs.

E 1071—6-Lt. Polished Brass.

Length - 96in.
Height - 6oin.
Width - 39in.

E 1364—6-Lt. Polished Brass.

Length - 96in.
Height - 6oin.
Width - 39in.

Plate 79

E 1307. Black iron and copper standard light with a traditional green silk shade.
The black ironwork is decorated with a copper bud at the base
and a copper ring on the neck. The height of the lamp
could be adjusted by loosening the copper ring.

E 1308. Black iron and copper adjustable standard lamp with
an orange silk shade. The column of the light grows out of
a copper bud set on the fitting's tripod.

E 1307—Black Iron & Copper.

Height - 54in.

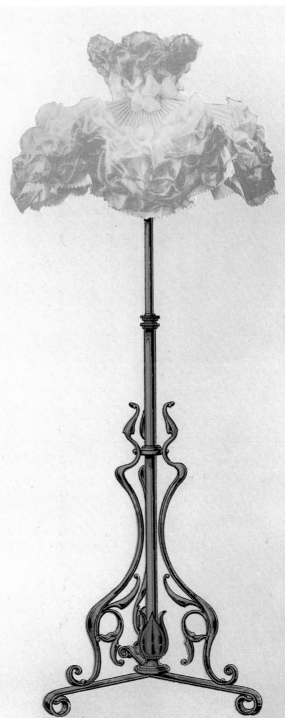

E 1308—Black Iron & Copper.

Height - 55in.

Plate 80

E 1302. Black iron and copper adjustable standard lamp with a green silk shade.
The black iron is decorated by the simple copper collar on the neck
of the column with which the height of the lamp is adjusted.

E 1169. Polished brass standard lamp of simple lines, set on a tripod.
The lamp is topped by a red silk shade.

E 1302—Black Iron & Copper.

Height - 54in.

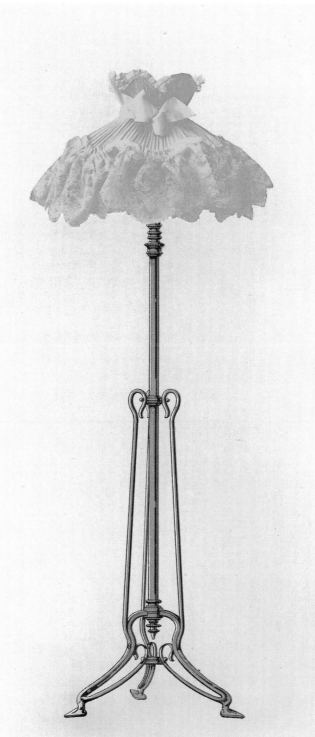

E 1169—Polished Brass.

Height - 52in.

Plate 81

E 1298. Polished brass standard lamp with a green silk shade.
Motifs based on the acanthus leaf are set above the tripod supporting the lamp.
Further leaf motifs are to be seen at the tops of the struts
that strengthen the lamp.

E 1296. Polished brass standard lamp with simple whiplash lines
and a pale blue silk shade.

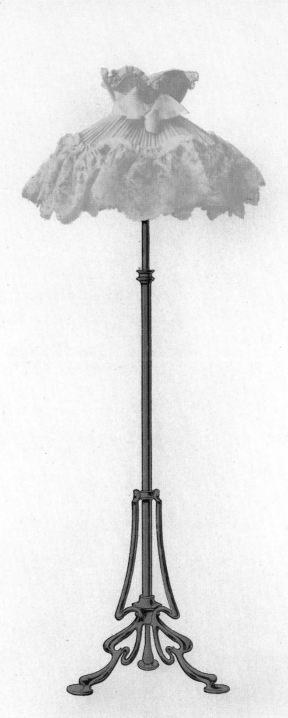

E 1298—Polished Brass.
Height - 52in.

E 1296—Polished Brass.
Height - 60in.

Plate 82

E 1299. Polished brass standard lamp with struts growing from the feet
of the tripod to form shoulders halfway up the column of the light.
The bulb is covered with an orange silk shade.

E 1042. Superb polished brass standard lamp topped with a crimson silk shade.
The cast brass and hand chased body of the lamp is formed
of a conventional Corinthian column whose base
is supported by four clawed feet.

E 1299—Polished Brass.
Height - 54in.

E 1042—Polished Brass.
Height - 59in.

Plate 83

E 1049. Polished brass standard lamp with an orange silk shade.
The simple structure of the lamp is decorated with griffin head motifs.

E 1297. Ornate polished brass standard lamp in the Empire style
with a crimson silk shade. The tripod is formed of animal legs
whose clawed feet clutch balls at the base of the lamp.

E 1049—Polished Brass.

Height - 54in.

E 1297—Polished Brass.

Height - 58in.

Plate 84

E 1300. Oxidised silver standard lamp with an orange silk shade.
A human face is set into the body of the lamp.

E 1301. Oxidised silver and copper standard lamp with a pale blue silk shade.
The copper is used to decorate the base of the lamp between the four feet.

E 1300—Oxydized Silver.
Height - 59in.

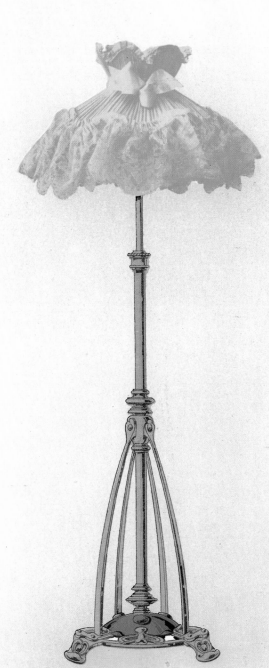

E 1301
Oxydized Silver & Copper.
Height - 59in.

Plate 85

E 1051. Exquisitely hand chased oxidised silver adjustable standard lamp
in traditional style with an orange silk shade.

E 1050. Ornate standard lamp in heavy cast and hand chased polished brass
with a built in onyx table and blue silk shade.
Table standard lamps were a common form
at the beginning of the century.
Some may still be found.

E 1051—Oxydized Silver.
Height - 54in.

E 1050—Polished Brass.
With Onyx Table.
Height - 54in.

Bibliography

Art Nouveau Style, Laurence Buffet-Challie, Academy Editions, 1982

Art Nouveau, Revolution in Interior Design, Rossana Bossaglia, Crescent, 1973

Art Nouveau and Art Deco Lighting, Alastair Duncan, Thames and Hudson, 1978

Birmingham Magazine of Arts and Industries, 1897, Birmingham Central Reference Library

Christopher Wray's Guide to Decorative Lighting, Barty Philips, Webb and Bower, 1987